Buddha in My Belly

Books by Brittany K. Fonte

Things I Never Want You to Find Out
Buddha in My Belly

Buddha in My Belly

Brittany K. Fonte

Hopewell Publications

Published by Hopewell
Publications, LLC
PO Box 11, Titusville, NJ
08560-0011
(609) 818-1049

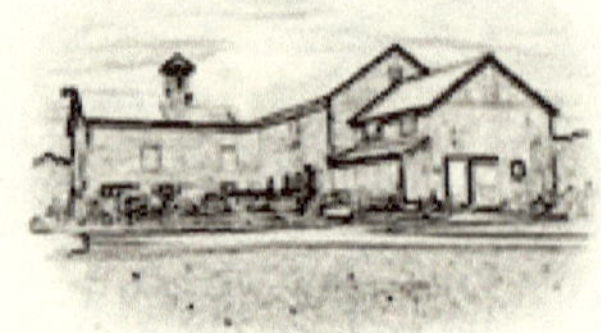

info@HopePubs.com
www.HopePubs.com

International Standard Book Number: 9781933435428
Library of Congress Control Number: 2012942542

First Edition
Printed in the United States of America

Poems in this collection have previously appeared as listed:

"Mommy Diet" in *Breadcrumb Scabs*
"Cinderella: 2011" and "I am not Fresh Produce" in *Mat Black Magazine*
"Bi-Cycling" and "Gidget's Unrest" in *Pemmican Journal*
"For the Masses Who Choose Spiked Kool-Aid" and "Roger Ebert: Two Thumbs Down" and "Forget You…and Forget Me, too, Cee Lo" and "Progress, Not Perfection" and "A Pattern Unworthy of Westminster Cathedral" in *Eunoia Review*
"Booksmarts are Still Silt at the Redneck Riviera" and "Call and Response" and "The Short Story" and "Runaway" and "Dear Professor" in *Camel Saloon*
Chapbook, *Things I Never Want You to Find Out*, from Silkworms Ink (UK)
"On Throwing a Stone from the Top of a Glass Building" and "No APA for What My Mama Said" and "Once When I Wore a Two Slim and My Stomach Was Flat" in *Writers Amuse Me*
"Why Prose Poetry?" and "She Sang, 'The Future's Not Ours to See…'" in *The Beatnik (UK)*
"A Seaworthy Epiphany" by *Quantum Poetry Magazine*
"10 Figs" and "Fifty Percent" in *The Legendary* literary journal
"Same Sutures" in *Marco Polo Arts Magazine*

For my sacred trinity, always:
Jackie, Jonas, and Keaton

Contents

SECTION ONE: PRACTICE

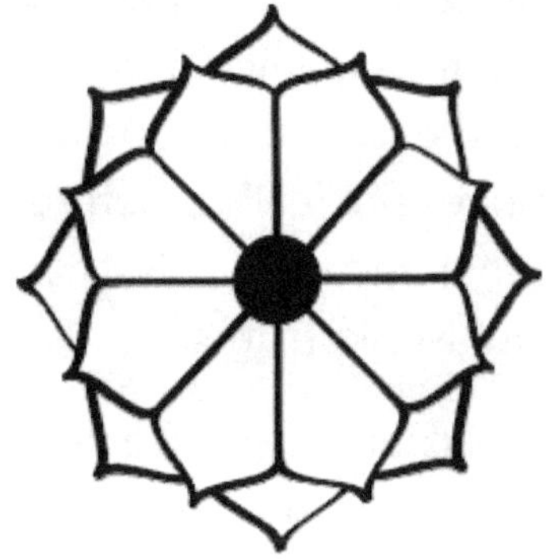

Directions for Zen

First, overfill an ancient (dead) family member's fragile teacup until sordid speculation rings your resuscitated wooden table and your crossed legs become one, ankle and knee, ankle and knee. Forget the fan above your head, flit, flit, flit; ignore the chink of clinking ice in the freezer door. Your rear, however cushioned, will regain feeling before the lesson is through, and your feet will finish fizzing when you swallow the Four Noble Truths.

Empty that teacup; yearn to have room for something more inside your head (more than media, mediocrity, melodrama) and something less in that heavy, saffron robe. Note not: Asians drive poorly, men love mildly, that starlet smokes weed, this neighbor steals mail. Block: my spouse has gained weight and my male child is meek. Meditate—even if you don't know how. Focus on emptiness, a brick-heavy topic with lead allegory: Just because you can drink tea from that cup, does not mean it is cup-ness.

Really recognize, "The grass is always greener... " is a proverb made by a man who wanted what he could not have until his wants weighed his face down in one-inch of filthy baby bathtub water. The phrase is not heard by those who consciously want what they have, or, philosophically, want nothing; wise men are deaf and poor. Think: It IS greener where a dog doesn't pee, where a car doesn't run, where an obsessive compulsive waters with incessant care, and fertilizes each spring, and uses homegrown, only organic compost.

Know: One should not speak unless it improves on silence. This, by our world's rules, though, only if you are not being subpoenaed, held at gunpoint, ridiculed, on a game show, phoning your ex, getting a test for myriad STDs or being asked, for the fiftieth time, "Do I look fat in this?" Speech is not just aural, but tactile, visual. A kind word can be a veritable kiss.

Lao Tzu said, "The journey of a thousand miles begins with a single step."

You: "But Jimmy Choo is not celibate, perhaps not straight. He does not sit beneath a Bodhi tree, but stands under an arch in a Parisian boutique. No sale on: heels, flats, daily wear, fuck-me pumps."

Tzu (maybe) "We are: barefoot at birth, barefoot in child's play, barefoot and pregnant, and we bare our souls as if they were more divine than the singing grasshopper, or his mute cousin."

The teacher reiterates, "You must first empty your cup."

You: "I paid $4.95 at Starbucks for this."

Subject: Dear Professor...

For Matt Ryan, my inappropriate hero.

I could not complete my weekly writing assignment because

a) my mother died. Again. It's been very hard trying to get her to cooperate this time and fill out the obituary; she says little and doesn't like to brag. I simply don't know what to say about her anymore. All the good lines have been taken.
b) my daughter is sick. She missed the toilet and threw up on the computer; it shorted. I have to go to the library to use their computer, now, and they don't appreciate my daughter's vomit.
c) I don't read English; I only write it. And not well. But don't worry; I'll eventually go back to my country.
d) it really is against my religion. I can only study Biology. I'm a Scientologist.
e) I don't want to upset you, but I know more than you do about the topic, and so I choose not to waste my time this way.
f) I believe the Rapture is coming. It's more important that I build my underground fort. I'll save you a few gallons of spring water. I'll throw in some Spaghetti O's if you can give me an "A."

g) well, it's top secret. I work for the government.
h) I'm a math major. I don't need to be able to read; that's what the admissions counselor said.
i) I'm only taking this class for the federal grant money.
j) I've read your poetry online. I don't want to end up sucking like you. No offense.
k) I've decided I don't need a degree to be successful, and so I've taken up nude modeling instead.
l) Um. It's difficult to say. I was unconscious for the majority of this week. I'm trying to draw attention to the college drinking epidemic. So far, I've got a huge following.
m) my Adderall pusher has been MIA. Or I can't find him because I'm too busy focusing on "Halo: IV" right now. I really like Coke products better than Pepsi products.
n) the reading assignment was inappropriate. I don't believe in multi-syllabic words or higher vocabulary. I prefer porn. With hot girls.
o) I've been working hard, training for a marathon. It'll be helpful in my neighborhood when the cops raid.
p) I forgot. I'm seriously the youngest case of Alzheimer's ever. I think that's what my neurologist said.
q) I haven't gotten my book yet. I'm not sure what happened; I ordered it at Border's.

r) I've been meditating. Any moment now I'm going to hit Nirvana and have all the answers.
s) I didn't think it was included in my tuition.
t) my dog told me not to.
u) my email isn't working. Or my IPhone. Or the computer at work. Or the library's cache of Macs. And I have no friends or family. I'm really a very solitary person.
v) I've been really preoccupied. My STD test came back positive. It totally explains the spot on my lip.
w) I took your directions literally. I DID complete the assignment; I just didn't send it to you. Should I do that now?
x) I had no time between my three full-time jobs, my physically handicapped spouse, my ADHD child, and the dog who wants to pee on every surface in my house, who also happens to be dying.
y) I was so awestruck by your beauty that I couldn't concentrate. Can I buy you a drink? Borrow you a prophylactic? Flunitrazepam? Offer you the key to my house? (Don't come by after 6 pm. My wife would kill me; she's said as much.)
z) I didn't want to. But I'm a recovering alcoholic. This is my amends.

(Pause.)

Type: "Dear Student…."

(Chin mudra).

Aristotelian Thoughts

Did I fall, he asked, preferably from a high place, from a place of social status and a world of wealth (did I fall, weighted with what would never be talked about, with what makes me a woman, maybe, what weeps.) Did I lose my moral meter or dismiss my rank, religion? He paused. I paused. The pain of literature and liturgy moved me to Ophelia origins, my dress dripping with the mass of marked denials I carry with me, always: human. My fatal trip was a true waste of Wang. I am, still, wet; my fate has been paid.

I couldn't say: "If I fell, my loss was my one wager: love. I chose to love a pace before me, to skip the solid lines between us like a blind truck driver, or Othello, to practice preaching patience, but bludgeon pews of mourners seconds before grief multiplied, single counts to minutes, mean.I bet my practice (re: relationship) would be perfect, my partner all she seemed in the subtle light behind primitive pink glasses, peace in our quiet, pleasure every time and priceless time alone, in bed, with leisurely meals and mealy leisure: the beginning."

So, your flaw…. He began. You say "potato" and I order asparagus. I was young and she was not; I was book-smart, heaving with heady hands on her hard-cut abs, absolutely relying on Braille to begin my married days. I saw her with sated hips and well-worn lips; I saw her in the night light and it was good. In six days, I fell. On the seventh, I rested in her arms, convinced, captivated, concealing nothing but that which I couldn't imagine in my flawed (see: normal) future.

Catharsis: I live in a home where pepper plants on window ledges wilt, die, dry up and flake. I live in a home where, no matter how much we make, there is always something out of reach: yacht club, hot bod, higher breasts, souls at rest. Lest we should forget, we should forgive our neighbors, forgive ourselves, forgive what we see in ourselves playing out in our lover's eyes; we should love others as we want to be loved. When we cannot offer such right change, we should see to changing to be "right." Like King Lear, we should forego favorites and favor fair.

Ah. Then, happiness is the meaning and purpose of life.

Yes, said Buddha.

10 Figs

Agriculture is hard, especially when you have brown thumbs, or no opposable thumbs at all, and hoes and hens are hard to find in India. But farming figs is a noble occupation, and Siddhartha taught more than: Figs grow on low-lying, open trees. Should you wish, or seek, sight....

1) Leave that fly flailing on the windowsill to its own devices. This fly fights, daily, just as you do; this fly has a right to his life reign, however dull, like you. And he will soon leave this life for another, perhaps a "higher," human form. (Your first child?)
2) That last cookie in the cookie jar just might not be meant for you. We should all avoid taking what is not ours, what is not intended for us: food, materials, sex.
3) Find the Middle Way when at the incredible Middle Eastern restaurant downtown, or at the upscale cupcake shop. Couscous will be fine four tablespoons in, filling with five, gluttonous past six; icing adds to an already crowded thigh, and mind. So much depends on one dream dish.
4) Slander is such that all persons involved hurt, post phrase. The one who speaks feels guilt, lacks

confidence; the one who is spoken of feels hate, then lacks confidence. Besides, people speak for themselves in the way they conduct themselves; speech is often unnecessary.

5) Indulging in alcohol is not about alcohol, or buzzes or sickness, but feeling moved to smash that fly, take that cookie, gobble that grain, and speak out of turn, too.
6) We should honor all faiths. We learn best that which is taught to us as children, and all faiths hone one rule: compassion. So it is of no concern who wears which church costume today.
7) Everything you do today, hurt or not, drunk or not, plants seeds for later feelings and actions: karma. This is not a deductible, not a sliding scale of payment, but simple cause and sane effect: elementary.
8) All life is suffering; we must accept and breathe despite this.
9) We all crave; we crave: love, attention, food, wine, children, money, power. But craving what we cannot have leads to suffering.
10) When we learn to want what we have, we are free.

Once, When I Wore a Two Slim and My Stomach Was Flat

Behind all the other memories in my walk-in closet is a pair of well-trodden jeans that never chose the right path, could not stop for maiming, knew no birds who spoke or iambic love-meter. These jeans hang, humble and humane, on a plastic hanger-of-long agos.

They know the scope of teenage want and the world of misdirected desire. They know the tug of peer pressure and the painstaking plodding of waking up too tired, showering with cold water, spending six thousand seconds on that perfect hairstyle and six half-minutes on goodbyes to family. Then, off to school: miles to go with silken patch, and miles to go before they trash.

A thousand nights ago I longed to wear those jeans— though "wearing" is a thing of their past and "pasting," perhaps, is more accurate. So much depends upon slim thighs, now; babies in red carriages juggle stomachs. I feel a lap band in my Brain.

That old jean's night I prayed that my gold wedding band stayed gold, that the fog of spousal screams would dissipate on tiny infant piggies, that we could build a bridge over our wasteland of: forgetting, distracting, believing, preparing, adieu-ing, and words potent as peripheral gun shots on a child-heavy lane in Suburbia, Tax Payers' Land.

She Sang, 'The Future's Not Ours to See'

If it rains (or we get caught lying on our taxes, taxing our mothers or mothering our spouses), we expect it to unleash an umbrella full of hail, and we are patients in the way that we undress to the sky, model soaked paper, bend over and expose all there is to know about our fears, inside. We wear galoshes humbly; we wear pleather precipitation hats made for '40's musicals. We watch the torrents on a weather map bleep by, cry, know there will be an end, then make plans for Tahiti next month (with tissues) and buy a skimpy bathing suit with which to woo a new mate. Maybe we meet with our counselor and sigh for one hour. We do not learn: dukkha.

If it's only cloudy, if there's just a hint of humidity frizzing our hair and nothing has shown up on the haughty radar yet (we don't know our boss has been checking our email, our identity's been stolen, we've forgotten who we are), we put our eggs in a generic faith carton, instead, and carry on like we've never dropped one before, spilled a yolk, cost a chicken a fortune in fertility drugs and an ugly reputation for being yellow and easy. We rage, later, against what seems unfair in that shelled mess and ignore: "What will be, will be." Silent is samsara.

When it's sunny—not a cloud in the sky—we imagine what's around the bend and forget to ferret away this Farenheit phase for another time, when it's necessary. We cannot stand still and rejoice in the rainless day, because that rain clouds our optimism, and those clouds cover rules of karma. We think, only, that sun cannot last, it won't end our days; it's solely sentimental, those seasonal rays. This, we cannot accept. So we pout. And we spin on our individual equators, spin away.

No APA for What My Mama Said

The fact of the matter is without citation in a copyright-centric world: Life is not fair. But the cruel joke in our universal human handbook is that it also goes on despite this. It goes on no matter how hideous an evening of stranger sex, how turbulent a custody situation, how ugly a slipshod facial surgery, how stupid a dire decision.

It goes on despite the unkind words of a woman who loves you, and to spite the kind man who's texting mute, who knows you better than you know yourself. He's seen you outside a mirror; he's known you outside of clothes and inside of twenty. He's built that plank of blind belief—and walked. You struggle for the life ring two decades too late and drown, wrong.

Life rolls forward, forcing regal, when an internal riot rips the best of your roots, and your mother is harsh, and your "father" is... not. It moves, snail time, when the light in the tunnel is flickering: train. And it skips twelve lines when the chorus is all that you know, and the audience reads lips, and your pitch pipe is priming pot, or oregano. (You wouldn't know the difference.) Yes, the spotlight is spent on moments this smart.

Life skips, only, if you realize: Confidence molds more than a strong set of shoulders; it carries more than a chest of minutia in a tattered T-back on a day without shampoo. This is the single strainer for the weight of the rest; this is the way through the world when your choice has turned sour and your words, soft, have curdled: satori.

When we gain years, we hope, we add fire to our stroke. If we do not, we use two sticks. We find a match. We blow on someone else's spark. We bend to a wind we cannot wield and worry less. Someone else's Mom: "It does not help."

Progress, Not Perfection

He, swaddled in calm and branded "better" by bare feet on a temple floor, starts: If Change is a river that swills differently every time you steep your toes into it, and if every atom in your body regenerates once a year, and if the knowledge you hold now is truly thicker than the pamphlet you held as a questioning toddler, surely there is hope....

Hope? She wonders if that river's pull can drown her in such a peace. She wonders if it stings like scotch, or cradles like vodka in the mouth, if it can wipe a slate clean like thirty days of community service, if it can teach her a skill that will support herself and her children and smooth the rocks of social welfare with positive propulsion.

He states: There is hope that you can be who you want to be, or who you dream yourself as already, despite the mirror image. There is hope regarding the façade of coming perfection your partner married, and then, noting the slow progression, silently resented; this is compassion.

She knows she can never be who she wants to be, not this way, not born into this body or this poverty or this country or this case of AIDS, or the need, each night, to down a bottle without a message, with a clear "Drink Me!" sign. She cannot fathom perfection, nor feel the chug of progress in section eight housing.

He says: There is hope that you CAN—by the time you roll, relaxed, downstream. Your reputation, like virginity, can be reclaimed after seven years of inactivity, even if you doubt yourself, now.

She can't remember the last book she read, or a time when her private parts were private. There's no time to read when she could be working. There's no need when you fill other people's glasses with forgetting and they leave dollar bills on tabletops because your hips are too broad for g-strings.

He senses her search and offers a grail that is not his own, or his people's: There is hope that you can find "you."

That night, she reads and reaches for spring water: If Change is that which cannot be held, then everything that has been born has already begun to die. And this is joyful. This is praise to the universe that pushes us to love as we can, now, because currents are swift and our foresight is fallible. We are human.

She puts down the bottle: beginning.

A Seaworthy Epiphany

It starts within a sentimental snow globe from a trip to Gloucester, Massachusetts (honeymoon). See: the weather is too cold for swimming and the blueberries have begged off for same-sex sleep. It starts with a solid principle that rallies all "lower" beings to higher good in polished glass: Let the lobsters go. (Commence shaking.) "That'll be $24.95," in the land of abolition and apple tea and picturesque precipitation—warm. This is a gift; I pack it, rolled in stolen, transformative towels, and move to lift off.

On tempest tides, through plastic peepholes and Reuters' mobiles, we seek these monks and nuns. Inside my suitcase, that holy water splashes in caving, curving walls—Americans playing at lama compassion in a world where welfare is considered a crime and leftovers are thrown out rather than levied for next life karma. Half-full of weighty intentions, we fly, transparent, out in the handmade whirlwinds of Eastern eggshell snow. Feet blessed in glitter, they collect cash, and cod. We order a vodka and cranberry.

Bland and open faces covered in scarves save themselves the need to stay stone-faced while pleading the lobster case; hands suited in fisherman gloves will never feed a town with just one fish, or take the time to use a Garten recipe, however easy. Instead, they solicit help from strangers who may or may not have ever eaten figs. They wheedle collections in weekday begging bowls for Wheel Turning Day, pat the bottom feeder who may have been our mother, our wife, in another, distant, life.

Beyond the theatrical and cylindrical world of perfect people/nature pairs protected in patent leather luggage and passion-stained cotton, we buy six hundred pounds of not-yet-red-crustaceans on ebay: PayPal. We keep our trans-Atlantic butter cold, save small (faux) forks for root vegetables and root for the under-seas, vicarious. (They unclip one claw and allow them to swim, freewheeling, wire-less.) The principle: We let the lobsters go to save them from us. But who saves the fish? (Turbulence threatens this tiny world, trapped.)

If Darwin Had Paid $20,000 a Year for His Son's Tuition...

High school antics and heads of gray hair worn thin by government jobs, and that jaded fog that comes with twelve plus years of a semi-sexless marriage, a steel-cut pre-nup, the best private school in the uppity county—post-recession USA—resurface: PTA. She taps her Mont Blanc pen on the guidelines for fundraising and controls her vision: away from the lies, open legs, liasons to boot-wearing Big Business in beautiful suits by breakout designers.

Here, she knows, there is protocol beyond the blathering bylines of CEO's who work 7-5 and 6-7; this is beyond the bread-breaking of women who have no idea how to bake bread, but can still order the best wine while whining about single mothers on welfare and wedge heels in French couture. While the years may show on the (untreated) foreheads of the fickle, the meeting-long text messages, sex-ages, e-complaints on too-soft speakers and too-fat features drip like expired milk cartons in uninspired lunch lines.

Personal private school protocol, of course, is clearly encoded in the cars that you drive, or those you loan to your babysitter to trudge the never-tethered heathens from home to school, school to equestrian practice, practice to counselor, grandmother, psychic advisor. Volvo and down: Keep your hands in your lap while the president preaches. Mercedes and up: Feel free to play footsie with the neighbor's wife, fellate the gym teacher, get fresh with the other mothers in the middle school class—just write a fat check for the endowment fund. Be sure it exceeds your hard on. It is not profound, but she is hated.

She is a less-than, wedged between the wear of well-used running shoes and a PhD to see: The Golden Rule is fluorescent, flickering. She knows the truth of humanity is closer to a survey confession of immaturity and couthe, this categorized 1-10, with 10 being Dalai Lama compassionate, 1 simply not running over the neighbor's cat on purpose. So when the meeting is over, and she hands the refillable pen to a puppy mill patient care manager, she knows: There is no evolution.

DMV: Department of *Moving* Vessels

She laments, "Oh my, Lord." It's Friday, at noon. She sits, ankles crossed, like a "good" girl in a church choir where they don't find frottage fascinating, or hidden cucumbers in retreat rolling bags. There are just two choices, both with fare; there are just two pedestals, equal in inches. One is beneath, and stable and strong; one's to the left, in the faster fate lane where the best super heroes (or strippers) grow into stay-at-home-moms.

From this philosophical Frost perspective, there is no balance of the bass of male, phallic to a fault on a synchronous score where a signature should be, but isn't, with the façade of the feminine, wily, shrill, sopranic in the piped-in, icing-to-life music all DMVs lease for waiting room wrist-cutting. From this view-point, she is virile, maybe, or feral; it depends on her choice. One stool: man-made, sturdy, matriculating the dependable missionary, and merits of lifetime loyalty. Another falters, creaks, comes when called, but instills fears of ass crashing—and sings as a Siren when she walks away.

She sighs, thinks she'll never see "next"—her number is 224 and they call, "Four?" Resigned, she scans a recent gossip rag, slightly soiled, beside her; love is a headline: "Unrequited!," "Undulating!," "Until Something Better Strides By!" And the far-sighted, hopeless romantic in the buttoned-up pea coat cannot see that the tripod beneath her, the culturally correct, the favorably fond, that ethnically-same, cavelling in congas gads long, fondling fantasies of *making* breakfasts for her bed and buttering respect to toast her with the best champagne a fat man can order is so... close. This will not hook a hooker, or handle the hard. This, though tried and true in its triad geometry, gains nothing when a challenge is offered.

Beauty is in the Eyes of the Baby Be-Holder, and Other Myths

Online there are a thousand photographs of childbirth-beaten bodies: bruised bellies, breasts, backsides widened by hormones and love, passionate mistakes and mistaken passion in the midst of an aching need for stability—whatever that means after intercourse. I forward these images, black and white, colored by female compassion, to friends who have had children or want to have children or dreamt of having children, once, but lost the fight with fertility and now bury themselves in work to ignore genetic ignominy.

Some of these friends are older, wiser; they carry their stretch marks like purple hearts and buy bras that perpetrate as old-fashioned jello molds. They know that there is nothing but scar-inducing surgery to change their mommy bodies, and so they humbly wear one-piece bathing suits, cover-ups, and befriend other wide women with baby battle fatigue. They pour their gelatin hearts into making their children as happy as can be in low-income housing or devastating divorce decisions, as well as their better bits, whom they love more now than before when they were be-muscled, not bemused. They know thirty pounds cannot undo thirty years. They are heroes, however heavy.

I send these portraits to young mothers, too: mothers who wore single-digit jeans before children, who still wear single-digit clothing after children, who feel their self-worth is only equal to their designer pant size, and that their pant size must be smaller than their shoe size in order for them to be loved at all. They love their children more than themselves, but make love to their spouses in the dark and buy cocoa butter by the gallon and, when they do gestate, do so with calorie counters and choreographed walks, leg lifts and nutritional guidelines meant for meditating ascetics. They read *The Pregnancy Running Guide*, though they've never run before, and will only realize they are beautiful when old age deals equality.

I do not send these pretty portraits to barren women, women who have lost their children, women who have lost maternal rights or only see their children on rotating weekends, women who were once men and have no wombs or are still fighting for the right to foster in their home states. They don't need my posts; these women would gladly paste such photographs to their skin, staple them, walk naked in the judging center of town. Thank God for their prizes.

For Pfizer, Who has Fortified My Family...

You are told that this is the magical moment you will remember forever ("Really!"), and twenty-four hours from now, too, when the nurse sends in the med tech to make you stand despite your major abdominal surgery and several days without sustenance. (This nurse is a mother; she knows it will hurt.)

You are told you should cry compost bins—because it's organic and politically correct—and praise a grandfatherly God when you're weighted in reckless doubt. You are layered in labor pains and leaking baby breakfast from between your lumpy legs; you are crying, but not as you "should."

You are told to look deeply into your physically comfortable lover's eyes (while not being able to move your own arms and not being able to feel your feet) and lean in for that cinematic kiss that will bond you together despite the insane sleeping schedule that will surely commence in just minutes. This is the domino to two years of fights, and the catalyst for clinically crazy and therapy bills not covered by insurance. This is resentment.

(Here is more than the pulling the male doctor promised.)

You are told you must take perfect pictures for faraway family and Facebook updates, regardless of your make-upped state, oily hair, black cue balls sitting in the deep pockets beneath your inky eyes. You must smile through the pubic pain and inability to pee and pounding temples to thank everyone in the room, no matter how callous they were when they cross-stitched your mightily overstretched muscles or whistled along to "Cold Play" as you worried if you would ever breathe again, or see your tingling toes.

You are told whatever name you've picked is beautiful, as the nurse wraps your goo-gobbled, personified part-time work in a straight-jacket swaddle. It's "Perfect!" even if it's "Chlamydia" (true story), even if it reminds everyone in your family of a foul smell or a fried appetizer from some third world watering hole. They let you write it on a dotted line days later, and traumatize a future teenager, because it would be rude to remind you that you are drugged.

When you go home, still heavier than some PMSing heffalumps, but apparently hospital "healthy," you are told to whole-heartedly embrace this coming time, as children grow too fast and you will someday miss the middle of the night cuddle sessions (also known as colic). You might also miss the size of your one-time mini breasts, your neighbor jokes. Your breasts grow to gargantuan proportions on the drive home, alone, and they continue to ache beyond the eternal ice packs and lettuce leaves and ibuprofen. You leak laboriously through your tight-fitting sports bra, cotton pads, terry washcloths. At night, mommy mammaries inhibit you from sleeping on your still spherical stomach, checkered black and bruised.

You try to be stoic against the "Ooooohhhh!"s and "Awwwwwwww!"s of friends and family because this is supposed to be the single most beautiful time of your non-sterile life—and you simply want to sleep. Solitary. You want someone else to cuddle your certainly wished-for, prayed-for, screamed-over, stuck-yourself-in-the-stomach-with-needles-and-took-pills-that-made-your-head-hurt-more-than-typical-migraines baby. This baby was almost two babies, too, because you knew there wouldn't be another chance; you almost chose the two-egg option because there wasn't enough insurance for another IVF try. You throw up thinking of twins.

The truth is, this miracle child has become a chore who screams with reflux and refuses to say "Thank you." No one can see this cherub child plotting against your once-peaceful life, ability to run five miles, ability to walk up the stairs or make a sandwich or take a shower with warm water, daily. This "angel" has moved your still-agile spouse onto the couch and, because you cannot see beyond your bandages, you don't know if you even have the material to have satisfying sex again.

You are told that the "baby blues" are only experienced by the mentally ill, and that Post-Partum Depression doesn't exist, and that medications like Zoloft and Effexor and Prozac are just pharmaceutical illusions created for weak women who don't really want to put in the work of raising wholesome children. You are told that you cannot complain about loneliness or pain to come, because your spouse will find another, more positive partner in the paces of parenthood. You must lose that weight quickly, because even the best of men need a visual jumpstart for their libidos. You are told that you are not good enough if you menstruate. Period.

On My Way to Where the Air is Sweet

"Sesame Street" is not the stuff of sexy dreams, sans the original and ogle-able Mr. Hooper, heart-open and retail ready; and five a.m. surely cannot be considered aphrodisiacal, even on New Year's, still in nightclub clothes, hurrying to hook ankles with necks and genitals with an ex (yawn). When babies cry concurrently with climax, the effect is less than earth-shattering and more like the end of a majority-heavy genocide on a futuristic Earth (fiction), flanked with half-dressed and Druid-ish aliens: Marvel.

And yet we expect this, this R-rated and randy Bert and Ernie routine, this slick-tongued Rosita courting our loins with letters and numbers (with fully ripe fruit for visual variety) on closed and current sets: singing, signing, swaying with rhyming. We somehow think that our thighs should tingle with theater of the absurd; there are elephants in trashcans—true. There are transient world travelers (blue), and metaphorical monsters, nude, with the pinkest of pink-tinted fur EVERYWHERE. They speak with Spanish accents, too, trilling tantric and teaching double entendre target nouns to actors in demure dressing gowns.

We still expect, as grown adults, as parents of children who chant Alphabet-ese with the ease we once lost earrings in the back seat of a taxi (us three!), that sex should come easy, should come often, and, because we have given up all outside sources of sexual satisfaction in serious and monogamous (read: REAL) relationships, our other halves should be better than the bragging we did as butt-bearing singles when anal was still "in" and outings equaled oral, reliably.

Oh, Telly! Teach me more than triangles and stranger danger; teach me that the languor with which I used to lick is not over. While I am covered in baby vomit, and while my (once willing) vagina struggles when the fussing starts in muted waves over mommy-monitors, I can still caress more than my own and dismiss the desire to dredge the perky past of power struggles and pinprick pasties and bartered quickies for my most precious hope. I can learn to tolerate what my partner cannot temper when sleep has tricked her, tripped her, traipsed out the front door, and I will feather my gigantic nest in R-reports of F-fair weather. Soon.

And Then They Bought Me a Car...

They said it wasn't my fault, this double fall from pheromone grace and step-by-step family phase out. I know it wasn't, as the spouses of alcoholics know they are not to blame for the temporary madness of a half-dozen shots of Sambuca, or lack thereof, on a bad business day during the week. I do not live in my parents' bed, in their festive fights on Christian holidays and memorable hours in between; I do live in the chasm of my surname, and it is something I cannot change until eighteen and able and in counseling with a therapist who suggests a fresh start is fated for the addict adult I will become.

He said he couldn't help it, rowing his penis into prep school ponds, and she said because he did, she did. Therein lies the biblical litany of stone throwing and platinum rules and pervasive social standards of American matrimony. I know that they are human, that they have weaknesses, but somehow children cannot fathom chinks in such oatmeal-spooning armor, or caveats of crossing the street holding the hand of a bigger person who babies you and yet belittles your second savior. I couldn't quite hear her when she said, "Sorry." I couldn't feel her bare ring finger reaching out.

So the conversation moved on from the bare threads of a hand-me-down wedding couch, sitting too still, to converting the garage, then gauging the cost of apartments in gaily-landscaped communities (near my school) of growing families that mimicked my own ten years previous. My mother, once "free," painted everything in the father-sanitized house, everything but the porcelain on the parenting pedestal sink, then got a job as some handsome man's secretary. I slowly understood that two homes only masked half the attention and a third the home-cooked meals (the third I learned to finagle out of frozen ingredients). My mother, once home all day, soon straggled home at sunset six, hair a mess, but "maid to no one." She was the boss on the other end of the bought-and-paid-for-cell phone at all hours of his unfaithful night.

Shallow Roots

Fear creeps in, at first, like the slight hissing of a goose sullied by coming weather changes and a toddler who drops mini crackers in a row, contrary, teasing. Compared to you, this goose is small; compared to you, this goose is downy, dumb. But he is not mute; and he can bite. This unsettles you: He helps you to rest at night, coercing in cotton, feathers fated for service goslings ago.

Fear comes, stealth, because you don't know your place in this world—a grain of sand among a beaten beach. It doesn't matter what you do, how you drown, tide in and tide out. You are just one of millions. You are no more important than the crab that displaces you, no more knowing. A handful of you only changes the land temporarily, only feels for the time it takes to climax; then it is still, between waves.

It pinches: sensitive skin in a zipper, floss in tight teeth, toes in too-high heels meant to elongate legs on women 5'2" and below who believe beauty is the quintessential ball of wax. It rubs like charcoal over fallen fall leaves, elastic-waist panties a size too slim, seasoning that will eventually slip off sweating chicken. It is a prick, the prick, pricking your finger when you don't know your HIV status, or being pregnant, one child already diagnosed: Prader Willi.

Fear is that tightness in your tender belly, that pulling in your pelvis at twenty-five weeks, only. Fear is not knowing that your child will survive, maybe because of fate, maybe because you never buried that far-flung hatchet beneath that allergenic Forsythia tree, never swallowed anger, never proctored peace.

Buddha in My Belly

My belly is bulbous, but empty; it's hollow with the hindrances of my wants in a world where I can never have enough chocolate chip cookies to fill my voids, where I can never void enough to make a preconceived model weight: 120. I crave and waddle through the wakes of long lost lives in aisles of sin, of choice. My cart squeaks a squall; it was not made in China, but Nepal.

I am ill-filled, still, after prayers and practice, patient meditation, prescription medication at the corner market; I am bulging with the brunt of what I think I should have, deserve, have earned, hoarded at a time when my family needed food and my frenzy fancied selfish fare: unfair. My blood carries such sustenance in sickly cycles because I cannot learn this; I glance at my list.

I know: I am pregnant with the work of the world, my world, the three-foot by three-foot invisible fence feigning the boundaries of "my" body. I search for something that might be mine in this realm, not understanding everything I have is on loan, EBT, even these 135 pounds I loathe. I search for produce, organic banana leaves, once-washed vegetables I can put on my table when the evening tithe is due, or thereabouts. I find coupons and my list, this scribbled on an origami crane; this prince is crushed by the weight of pinched and peripheral pennies:

Flour

Oatmeal

Rice

Melon (bitter)

Ita palm

Nori

Endive

(I forget: Lotus root, figs.)

Despite my list, at this grocery store I want carbs. I search for sugar; I take more than my arms can carry for clandestine, nightly meals with...me. Only me. I cannot balance scales or scale back the material for the maternal, alone. I cannot face a scale or I.D. my feet beyond my fat. Not today. Aisle One: a carnivorous call. Two: spicy seasoning. Three: everything is grievously gluttonous. I know old age, disease, death beyond my palace walls. I glance at the pharmacy counter, cold.

Brittany K. Fonte

When my cart is full, filled with my humanity and mental malas, when the Safeway Club Card is tired of fighting fate and fickle tomatoes (fruit, or?), my stomach calls: nature. I cannot translate, so I try and tickle, only, the surface of that Buddha seed, a grain of sand, a grin in the making that I made when I loved. (I breathe.) Now, I love the world so much that I will give it my only child. I look around me, match my Middle (Way) with others': He is present in us all.

SECTION TWO: HUMILITY

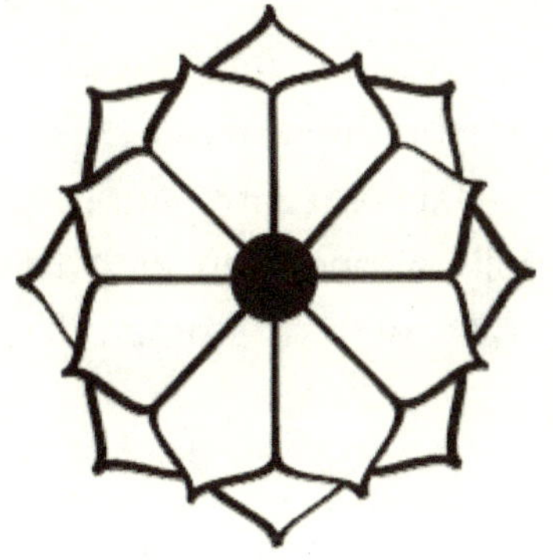

I am Not Fresh Produce

I am graying and thirty-three; I am pushing forty and other people's borders and the reflective guidelines of decency in pajama pants, also a rickety motor home/stroller/carry-all cart in the produce section of an organic market. My infant claps her dimpled hands—unaware of those dimples, unaware of her footed sleeper—at teetering apple pyramids. She screeches joyfully at the man with the microphone who cannot talk with a human lilt, but smiles, anyway.

This man is here several times a week. He enjoys the children who do not cry at his robotic voice, or those who do not laugh.Throat cancer beat his esophagus, but it did not tame his indignant optimism. He hands out coupons to busy moms and elderly couples; he hands out dollar bills to homeless men. He sips coffee from earth-friendly paper cups because he does not, cannot work for this store of twenty-something vegans with titanium-filled cranial holes.

I know I should learn the lesson he is here to teach, because I was a philosophy minor, and my middle-class privilege expects I dry-hump all that is logical and modest, masculine and old. Still, I feel my too-ripe stomach inching just a thumb's inch over my too young jeans. I pick up an avocado and molest its brown skin, wishing I had the money and the contacts to slice my own mid-section crosswise, like I'd do to such fruit to make guacamole: Use a spoon to carefully remove the soft fat from the beaten pleather, discard a hard seed, pack the remaining flesh into a concave mold with ingredients that make me suck my cheeks in naturally.

I'd tell my wife: Spoon me. I'd direct: Press harder HERE. I'd stay green for fifteen minutes, then be eaten. Whole.

When the man with the cancered past and the Servox asks me if I am interested in the mangoes today, I flinch, too fickle and feminist to disregard a kind man's innocuous comparison. I want to tell him: I'd rather ripe tomatoes. I'd rather small and tight, unbruised—something that juices when you nibble it. Something that mates well with vodka and yearns for unpasteurized goat cheese. I want to point to the bright plums, then ask him when he started smoking and if he'd taught his children.

Instead, I grab my list from my child's mouth:
Bananas
Papayas
Pineapple.

For Little Girls Once Dressed in Pink...

At what point do you give up, give in, decide to give less because there is nothing to gain from the give-and-take of a relationship that is teeter-tottering (he is heavier) and was over before it began?

And what does it take to balance that playground toy, sanded as it is with: a disrespectful word, a scowl, a slap, a missing punctuation mark from one night, one party, one swinging compromise: rhythm method( )

When you are sixteen, and the world seems to spin on a carousel of shopping and proms, the sting of a butterfly needle hurts as much as an abstract idea—and for as long. You might think: STDs, baby, babies, OUCH! But once that needle is extracted, so is that terror. Your stomach is still flat; your sometimes-boyfriend says he's soooooo sorry. That prick is just the past, and you've applied a band-aid.

The test was free at the clinic, but when it comes back positive, you know "free" won't cover formula, diapers, toys or a crib. "Free," even "cheap," is a train's ride away from that senior trip to Prague, or your missing papa's home in the Big Black Hole. You'd get a job, but it would interfere with cheerleading practice; you'd have to pay your parents for gas. You hope OB/GYNs work on a sliding scale.

You ignore it, the baby grain of sand, then jelly bean. Three months of throwing up and your mother thinks you're bulimic; she asks you if you think you're fat, if you've been reading her *Cosmopolitans*, if you'd like to talk to a nutritionist or see a personal trainer at her all-women's gym. You think, if you only wanted to look at naked, overweight women, you wouldn't be in the predicament you are now. You eat hot chilies, parsley, Blue Cohosh. You jump up and down every chance you get.

At five months, you tell your best friend—a gay boy with his own issues—and he uses the term 'breeders' before he admits, "That sucks." He plays your mother in a dramatic rendition of you, spilling your guts, even telling about the date rape incident, holding nothing back. He asks, "How could you be so irresponsible?" You can tell him, "He's hot," and "He said he loved me," but you won't be able to tell your for-real maternal figure.

You decide you cannot do it alone, this naked tail-telling. You ask gay Jermaine to stay, to sit next to you at dinner, to interfere, physically if necessary.

Brittany K. Fonte

Over omelets and hash browns, dry toast and pulp-free OJ, you whisper, “I’m having a baby.” Your mother is deaf; you say, louder, “I’m pregnant. I’m sure.”

Your mother leaves the table, one hand over her mouth; you will do the same in sixteen years. Your step-father stands as he did when you were five at that park, and the long wooden plank with the broken handles and the split seat crashed down down down. You hurt: round ligament pain. You cry. In four months you’ll ask for an epidural, alone.

Cinderella: 2011

For A.G.K. and K.E.F.

I married young in a rabid display of hierarchical power and alcohol advertising; there were no other options for me: a pretty girl with no education and feral feet with crazy high in-steps. I knew I wanted to be known—to try my hand at limb modeling, maybe commercials, maybe acting. I didn't know that marrying a man I hardly knew, however hung and gorgeous and rich, would turn out to be a tiara-ble problem, political et al. So I wished for it fervently, then acted the rosy-cheeked bobblehead and squished my size-eight feet into a petite pair of glass pedi-pads when the wand came down.

There are no couples' counselors in Happily Ever After, and if there were, a prince's health insurance surely wouldn't cover weekly meetings or Zoloft or the time it takes to pull my "handsome" husband off his just-for-show and visiting-toothless-(horny and desperate) peasant-women ivory steed. It wouldn't cover the drama necessary to pack the kids off to Her Highness Nana's, the oats to drive to the next kingdom and argue the way back over about who said what, kept what, distorted all, and why, when I said, "I do," I said "I don't" to blow jobs and rear entry loving. It wouldn't make me forget that other woman's smell on my husband's white, embroidered lapel, or ignore her panties in the ball gown glove box of the pumpkin Prius.

I married young—twenty-one—and the tabloids saw it as a dream come true. They noted I wore Vera Wang and Jimmy Choo; I had a train that knew no bounds and, with two bitty words and a tongue-less, pristine kiss, the exclusive rights to a kingdom without end. What they didn't say was that I'd never dated any man before, and had only ever seen my father and his Sunday caddy pulling clubs behind them as they left on Monday afternoons for the local tavern, the cathouse, the pharmacy.

I was naïve, my manual on man education without an index, without pictures and diagrams and penile instructions, without promise; my mother died when I was young, leaving me no happy housewife handbook, never giving me sex talks or morning-after prescriptions for that first, tumultuous tenure of marriage. Before my fine sand slipper gala, I had resigned myself to a life of servitude in a dying cleaning business my step-mother owned on the wrong side of town. I had decided that washing windows whittled my waist and scrubbing floors felt virtuous. The birds understood. They built their nests each spring in my attic, despite my ne'er conditioned hair.

But I fell for that ideal of a rich husband and a set of servants. I fell after two margaritas and a glass of Shiraz and some rolled paper that probably swaddled stale oregano. There was a gay man, prettier than me, who wore gossamer wings and gave me a MAC eyeliner pen in the alley next to the "Clean as You Go" office; he told me to buy some Style Snaps and raise my skirt to properly frame my cat. I gave in to that ignorant voice in me that pleaded for something more than Windex and Mr. Clean and Endust to end all dust in those dark and forgotten crevices that only spoke during '90210' and close-ups of Luke Perry; I gave in with my tithe of one intact hymen, and learned a new in-bed vocabulary from a variety of internet sites. I got breast implants and Restylane and took pole-dancing classes with the other frigid maidens of the Merry Endings Moms' Club.

I got divorced.

Fifty Percent

I say, "I think I want a divorce," as if I've thought of anything but in the time it took to call a sitter, kiss goodbyes, get in my car and drive to this office, felled like a tree out of hearing range just waiting for the woodsmen to strike with chainsaws much superior to my broken bark heart. I speak as if there's any choice in the matter of One vs. The Other, or Doormat vs. Boot Heel With Strong Left Hooker. It's hell inside a beaten mind, and I can't hold in the fated flicker any longer. I hold my breath when I lie, and I am running out of air. There's no cover up that can defy the portrait of a prisoner who falls down steep stairs once a month.

The lawyer smiles a smile that is not nearly as compassionate as I'd like, but it's cogitating, collected, and clearly practiced in the photograph she's pasted in the community column; she could win. I know: It is more than banal bickering and more than bitchy barking. It is more than nodding without listening or yelling without forethought at children who've not yet found their "off" buttons or volume switches. This is more than throwing frying pans with spatting oil, too. If I perjure, please—give me solitary; I cannot keep the tears from furrowing, frank, when my left arm is twisted: to stay, to serve, to conceive, to break when the right answer is forged. I do not believe this is the way; I have seen reruns of "I Love Lucy" and heard love songs by Lennon.

There's tension. I break. It's not her; "It's me." That's what I thought when I burned dinner that first night, broke the television, televised an argument at breakfast with my sister who would say too much, wore ripped jeans lipping low on my hips and won a black medallion "...walking into a door." It's what I whispered when I couldn't come, and offered when that man stared at me as if I'd known him, carnally. I admit it was me: I decided to stay because I was pregnant and jobless, believed I could change the person I loved like Lazarus. But I was dead, too.

I say, "We have children," because we do. Two. But when I say such aloud, my sanity gurgles and my past intentions make their way from my fettered stomach through a tense trachea. I feel acidic failure spout up in my mouth; there is vomit for five years of faking it with teachers and neighbors and Child Protective Services' calls in response to my neighbors. There is bile for (voluntary) exile from my family. I know fear. I offer my time here on earth to some god, now, and then I shake like the surface of a lake leveled by a tiny skipping-stone, alone: skip, skip, skip, sink. (((Rings.)))

The lawyer, who probably would rather be called an attorney, hands me a piece of paper with her professional fees and pertinent information. It's black and white and I like gray. It's heavier than anything I've ever held, louder than what I'd say, and newly copied: The ink is wet. Hours and handfuls of zeros seem to cohabitate in columns that begin with "If..." and end with my keeping my children, my life, my name. Money can't matter, now. I know the bitterness of an argument on my tongue, the taste of loss and lost fillings, both. I nod. I don't have it, but I will. Will. I approve her numbers because there's no choice today, and there's no option tomorrow.

When the attorney discovers my spouse is a "she," she pats me, maternally, tries not to be patronizing, explains: There is no law for that, here; there is no precedent. I could call the police and file a protection order, but then my children would be without health insurance, tuition, college funds, food; I've thought of this. My kids would be without access to their second mother, without housing or hope as the seeds of second-class citizens. My lungs ache to capacity with the scream that has been building bimonthly with my brutal brandings and a fairytale world at odds for more than the time DOMA has been in place, for more than the length of Gaga's career. My hands sweat with knowing: I tried a treaty at home. The fact is that my facts don't matter to a Family Coalition who protects anyone but children who have two mothers, one mother/ no man, idealized couples with unfaithful, rich CEOs. But I say, "Thank you." I feel the chainsaw. And I am shown the door, again.

The Perfect Pair

It had been months, at least, since they'd had sex, and the last time had been so perfunctory, so planned and painstaking, that she'd barely panted, had not taken off her shirt, and, when she got up, she went straight to the grocery store. (Her hair was still coiffed and her list was nagging her beyond thoughts of post-coital cuddling.) There, she bought salad fixings and consciously resented her lack of orgasm while fingering firm produce.

She knew she was older—52—but her body seemed as hard as it had ever been, her breasts as high. She still modeled, even, and was often seen in bathing suits, glittered fairy wings, ballerina costumes and ball gowns on the cover of international media. Her husband modeled, too, but was less successful than she was and, sadly, not as endowed as either of them would have liked him to be.

They'd never had children, both of them infertile, but they had adopted her little sister, Kelly, and, in this way, felt fulfilled as parents throughout their thirties. When Kelly went away to college, and then veterinary school, their empty nesting began. They had to learn how to reengage with one another, how to see that they, in fact, were, literally, made for one another. Often the pressure of being Mr. and Mrs. was too much, and they would retire to separate bedrooms in their Dream Home, with separate television remotes.

It did not come as a shock, of course, when she found out he'd been with someone else. And she should have known this someone else would be a man. She had tried so hard to keep as trim as the first day he met her, to bleach her grays and laser her legs. She had succeeded in looking 21 forever, and even this hadn't turned his head; everyone but she had known he was gay from this fact, alone. She tried to tell him, "We can see a therapist, Ken."

He simply shook his hard head, gestured to a man beyond their home in a pink convertible (a man who, oddly enough, looked just like Ken, only blonde) and said, "This is who I have always been, Barb."

The Short Story

SETTING: Many weeds grow green in the Midwestern wilds of cows and plains, mosquito-filled lakes and conservative politics. Wisconsin happily barters in cheese curds and whey (sown by serial killers), the twin Dakotas dapple in deer ticks, dust and durable durham wheat. My Minnesota, though, touts corn and soybeans, also gun racks, goys, and cheap ale. Ice fishing holes, sans crops, are stuffed with mammal heads and hookers as company-come-tail. I was raised here, shallow soil et al. "Gay" meant "jolly," only in the way it was used in famous Broadway musicals recreated at the local (Norwegian) rec center. Here, lefse is rolled as much as Mary Jane, and Mary Jane marries men.

CHARACTER: Mary Jane married three men, maybe high, but I hoped for more. I held Ellen a hero without a hampering cape, or male hormones. Nineteen and nit-witted, I coddled visions of karaoke love songs in my mind of minimal focus and teetering tone deafness. Feeling powerful with temporary parental leave, and teenaged volcanic panties primed in electric shocks, I panted after—preyed—on pretty coeds without guilt, without redneck perceptions, concepts of "perversity," or narrow-minded prattle. Until.

THEME: Until Eternity: This is what I promised her. I kissed her once, offered, "Until we meet again." Until the clock struck twelve and my spring break curfew counted; I held her hips until the cows came. I thought of her driving home, got a speeding ticket from a dyke who couldn't see me for who I wanted to be. I thought: Until the fat lady sings. Until the end. Later, I told my parents until I was blue in the face: I love her. Juliet and Jolie-Pitt. They were silent. They wouldn't accept it, not until Hell froze over. Sex equaled guilty until proven guilty.

POINT OF VIEW: Guilt from Her. Mom. The old-fashioned. The bigoted. The Christian Right. The Focus on the Family, not mine. The Majority. The Man. The Commandments. The hope for a grand-child. The neighbors and what they might say, have said, have seen over a privacy fence. The hurt I might contend with. The discrimination. The "phase." The idea of tab A and slot B without silicone accoutrements. The slut. The family friends who will not accept me. The façade. The children with no father. There is, also, God.

PLOT: My God, Thanksgiving came gifting and I, riding shotgun in my mother's shuttle van, thinking of tofu turkey and brown buttered biscuits (basic human rights) showed my cards: I shouted, "I'm in love. With a woman." Torrential, tyrannical screams ensued, and then my ride was wrought with the most soundless of nauseated silence.

It was clear I would not break breads of bartering, then. There was not one loaf for all, and I had to bide my time until a foreign taxi could return me to sender, reset my sexuality, tally all of my wrongs as a child. And all of my tuition costs.

CONFLICT: The cost is more than I have.

Euripides Threw Me Under that Bus, There

In a dark, dreary corner of literary history, Greek, there are two dead children chosen to speak for revenge and machismo and the (believed or perceived) inbred faithlessness of handsome men with more money than sense: drachmas. She scrubs this corner clean, her chore for the week; her cellmate writes letters to senators.

Some say these children were killed, mother conscious; some say they died of a devastating look—away. Some say the citizens of Corinth began this: break Medea, bury her sanity, board up her loins. Euripides decreed: Medea killed her own children, driven by vengeance, forgetting her motherhood. "How can you forget?" she thinks, signing up for Aunt Mary's Storybook Program.

The damage done, in media and maddening mirth, her name means murder. Her name means more than castration by frustration, bludgeoning by passion, suffocation: Buy feather pillows (hint: down dims death sounds). Her name suggests a child is a tool in a marriage to a tool, and that it works to kill for care. But hearsay is close enough to heresy to claim an appeal.

(Book closed.) What Euripides did not show? Medea's love for Jason: raped, sowed, abandoned. Here, today, humans are fallible. Fate, perhaps, is feigned. Grown-up love might mean more than a woman who weeps over breast milk, depressed, ill inside. And old, dead men might have been chauvinistic. Might be, now.

Parole hearing: 2025.

Identity Crisis?

I recognize that I am Caucasion; this is a genetic disorder I cannot control, propagated by Norwegian fishermen and Irish milkmaids who wooed one another over large mooing mammals and married in a Catholic church not far from Minneapolis (despite their Lutheran heritage). I cannot control, either, the country I was born into, the middle class family in the MidWest with an above median income, and the opportunities, therein, for higher education. I have been blessed with a fiscally and physically comfortable marriage. Our son goes to private school. Our babysitter makes much over minimum wage and has a Master's degree; she is Caucasion, too.

I know I am Caucasion despite the centuries old Black Irish lay-over in curly-Q frizz. When I look in the mirror, in the very expensive house with the uppity nautical city behind me (I own a sailboat that sleeps eight and belong to the Yacht club—this is why I have my hair professionally straightened, monthly; this is why I faux tan), I know I have been given more than my share of the Communist pie with a petite nose and whittled rear and Pecola blue eyes. My religious background begs me to embrace the guilt of so many material hoarders before me. I try to cry for Dear John Paul, but the Botox restricts my forehead and the nose job makes sniffling hard; besides, tears would mess up my mascara. My extensions frizz when wet; when my body does not, I can buy K-Y. (Or this is what you think.)

This is what you think, when the truth is what most in this world cannot see, at least not until I'm naked, stark, with another woman above me speaking a different love language, is that I can hallucinate poverty and racism, addiction and illness. It's not tattooed on a visible body part—there are those who might judge me white trash—but I can look into my daughter's eyes and feel what it's like to love another being simply because she lives and breathes and needs as I do. I've eaten faithful figs against that bodhi tree, and I know that her eyes could be yours, in another time, in another place. Her eyes could be brown, or blood shot or sparkling and slanted. She could be a fly that I shoo outside instead of swatting inside, dead. It doesn't matter in the grand scheme of Nirvana, and it won't show in my winter-white and well-fed gait. I do not take communion. Siddartha said, "The divinity in me sees such in you." I listened.

So while people may judge my belief in the words I wear on my size "implants" T-shirts, while they might see my 5k run for homelessness as a quick way to burn off calories from caviar and champagne, while I may wear high-end clothes when lecturing a women's group on the dangers of racial and economic prejudice in a diversified community of mostly white, mom-and-dad-and-two-kids-families in multi-million dollar homes, I know figs equal feeling. I know, even though I have not ever hungered beyond what Weight Watcher's has skimmed from me, even though I have not waited on a corner for a bus or a pimp, a social worker or probation officer: I cannot live in any colored human skin without wondering if others are comfortable in theirs. I give Ahimsa. I pray in gray, and poor, and gay.

When Palmolive Doesn't Clean the Pelicans and Anti-Bacterial Soap is Mud

A perfect circle is harder to draw than one with once-pretty sides flattened by age, or heat, or glass pricks with impeccable aim and worse-than-teenaged-anal-sex timing. It is pristine, like a nun's fortress-of-faith ring, and unending as a hidden mental illness, without health insurance, or nearby clinics, or family who cares where hell might reside. It is consistent: the rants of an uneducated racist, armed, near a sea of real democrats in a sweeping bread line in downtown D.C.

A circle—one stroke, no stops, bare and bucking—demands respect. When we cannot get it right, as humans, we suffer the humiliation of simplicity beating (barren) patience. We throw the pencil across the room and "Fuck!" all that is difficult that crossword day; we slip on the bath water, miss the bar, ignore the baby. We give up, give in, give hope to that invisible space in the center of the room where an argument hovers, hangs in rough rope, still unclear, the place where the bruises begin to purple and her confidence pauses for breath.

And if we, even wrestling with a tangible protractor, cannot draw that perfect orb, we must admit so much more is beyond our greedy grasp: snowmen, cartoon eyes, halos, planets, condoms, pupils. Then heaven, love, purity, wisdom are square, rare, past and pruned to death under the thumb of desert thirst. We cannot carry the baggage of beauty with bedraggled circumferences or lopsided stones cast by custom, even here, even now.

Children cry at the seemingly simple task; artists sigh, set their paints or pens or photos down to drink, instead. This is because we know, if a perfect circle is so impossible, peace is possibly extinct. Love cannot be what it seems on a cloudless day. Our hands cannot be washed.

On Throwing a Stone from the Top of a Moral, Glass Building

For Jackie. Always.

Step. Step. Step; step, step.

Step. Step. Step step step.

The fifth story: I've climbed up here, via Weight Watchers activity points and a guilty, gut-jiggling conscience, to be alone with myself and my thoughts and someone else's ideas about who I am or must be, now that I am in my thirties, peri-menopause threatening, my best-looking years behind me waving curtly and somewhat embarrassed from the window at Abercrombie and Fitch.

I am here, dressed in mom-jeans that swallow my hefty hips, whole, and a (black) turtleneck that denies the existence of collarbones, breasts, a waist—everything but my chin-thickening, teeth-crumbling, cute-as-can-be children. I wear hole-created underwear—the kind that covers my criss-crossing C section scars with thick "Hanes for Her" elastic—and an underwire bra that leaves a pinched inch all alone, dimpled and denied bra entry, scratching against the rough cotton of said baby puke stained shirt.

I long to disregard my domestic identity, levied as it is with water weight, warring cleaning supplies, wallops of want beneath the broad, daylight-streaming skylights.But I lack the maternal dictionary that celebrities use, along with the stylists, make-up artists, personal trainers, chefs and connections. I sit alone, self-help book still closed on my Oprah-channeling lap, craving calories that will only couple chastely with fat cells when I sleep, that will only texture my tummy and try my temper for seventeen-year-old swimsuit models with budding bimbo breasts and boutique shoes.

Pad. Pad. Pad; pad pad.

Pad. Pad. Pad pad pad.

The fourth story: I've wandered down here because they've put out a free continental breakfast. I can walk past the donuts—they appear to be cream-filled and I don't care for cream—but other carbs court me, crying. There are bagels with peanut butter panting a 900 number pant; there are pancakes and potatoes and French toast ménage et trios-ing. I drink coffee with whole milk and saccharine-free sugar, knowing I will regret the choice later, think about wretching, find the idea too revolting (or difficult) then decide I've already killed my diet and eat two pints of Ben and Jerry's—on sale at the Safeway 2/$7. I take a new, sparkling plate every time I visit the venerable breakfast bar (various times), leaving the old, bedeviled ones behind on other people's dirty tables, stealth.

Pit. Pit. Pat; pit pat.

Pit. Pit. Pat pit pit.

The third story has an open women's restroom; I've had too much caffeinated coffee and my bladder's been perforated by two pregnancies. I close myself into a safe stall to breathe for a moment, to muscle my self-confidence into being. But when the door is closed, I cave; I eat the M&Ms I've stashed in my purse for children in long lines or car rides down the short street. I can count the ways in which I hate myself, as I hear the tinkling of wee woman rain on my right, my left, and, beneath the partition, see the dripping drip drip of a poorly constructed, stainless steel sink. Heartburn stings, as do: unrealized dreams, spousal regrets of religious proportions, drying desire, hair that won't straighten, a forehead that folds, spare fuzz above lips and eyes and ankles.

I take the elevator to the second floor, sad, unsoothed by my stash.

The second story: It's at least a Celsius degree colder than the other three stories. I reach for my sweater, rolled into a whimpering ball in my once-pristine, now juice-covered, purse. The tag has been torn out, the "L" a reminder of the size of my boy-like bones and one-time heart. The re-circulated air smothers me, as do the salient fingerprints suffocating the floor to ceiling windows. I should be at my desk. I should be editing technical reports and returning phone calls, but my mind is too full for details. I think: I cannot lose. I enumerate: spouse, family, respect, trust, status. But I have. And bottles, mops, lullabies and chauffering cannot buy them back.

C r a w l.

In the basement, I drop my bag. I ditch my sweater; I forget how to breathe. I finger my eyelashes and slip off my beaten Target-brand tennis shoes. I find a corner where the baseboards are almost clean and huddle, my head in my thighs, my arms hugging shins of sins.

There is nothing but pebble, here.

Call and Response

Two rings, then three. (Serendipity?) She, in Chi town; he, in their town: Both hold space with desperate arms, alarmed, facing fifteen years of macramed marriage, and fears of losing an identity (or even that *inkling*) they created before regular sex, baby cravings, whittling siren-sex, that ex, careers of consequence. . . .

She wonders, whiling while tones tone in a loaned hotel room of well-loved beds, if she can be content, alone, with one man; he can never be all she needs. Cannot. As fish need more than a tank, her heart sank when he forgot: her birthday, their anniversary, the condom, milk. He is not a chef, and is not Hugh Hefner.

But there are never three in such a first world country of Christian zip ties and Velcro marriages, bold-faced lies of *Mrs.* and *Ms.*. There can't be three while the pope still breathes; the tethers of Steinem-feminism miss Lincoln's nose, picks bare, there.There cannot be three, meant to be, while two boast such a lofty percent: 50. But she knows men.

She knows 50%, surely, is more than what should be, must be behind locked doors, just as those sex surveys roar: Mothers—even whores—do not make love three times per week, not even alone. There is simply no time to moan with Jif and jam, drop off and pick up, soaps and stones, rinse and dry. Dry. She knows, three rings in, he has company. She casts a line to fantasy, too.

Then, "Yeah?"

His common syllable darts, starts a chain of Cain images. It's quiet. Jizz-us. His mind flits to cover: that old girlfriend from ninth grade and her blonde mother, the swimsuit model from France, the Fed Ex woman's tight pants, the front man and teenaged stage hand of the metal band he saw—just once—live, also a few lines from a do-me movie he paid $8 for when he couldn't get laid. His wife often had a headache.

She says, "I'm here. Safe." And the miles weight her haste to get to once-hidden alone time, "Me Time," the mini bar or a drink at the open bar without the children shooting par into porcelain vases, or cleaning Sharpie mazes—on the wall—and a hungry husband. A dozen pared phrases and that's it. Shit. Is there nothing he can do? (Sigh.) "Love you."

"Yes." And he IS happy, means his merry sign off, even while mind-mapping the miles that stand between him and Hollywood, him and his truant, television third.

Bi-Cycling

Not women?

It's darker than it should be to sit on a bike that wobbles by nature and goes nowhere with a non-day-glo odometer; like the tree falling in the woods that no one cares about hearing, I am pushing and pulling my legs and hip flexors to physically afford Jimmy Choo shoes so I can fuck a man, or teenage-dream it, in $800 pumps that my wife pays for selling drugs.

(Drugs: on the corner of a time-slipping ant-farm. In an office building with real marble floors and faux particleboard partitions between fickle receptionists: Hair up? Hair down? Sleep with the boss? The mail boy?

These are drugs you can buy generic with a co-pay, drugs that may save your life, and will certainly take care of that pesky constipation from all those chemo treatments. Drugs my mother-in-law who isn't, and can't be while a Republican has hypocritical control, didn't have a chance to take and so she stopped. Living. Was stopped up when she stopped living. Those drugs...)

It's echoing moans and grunts and smelling rank exertion in the public exercise cave. It's spinning porn and sensual torture and social guidelines pen I'm not allowed to talk to my neighbor. I am thinking about that waspish actor whose boy pliers I'd pay to needle-nose, and I am learning that I can push that tension up, ratchet it more than the instructor says above her eightie's rock and Newton-John legwarmers.

I can handle the spin and "Rocky" theme song as I think of ways to impress upon my wife that my prime time fantasy life is more vivid than the way she remembers her last drag, the drag she can no longer take because she works for a company that will afford me neutral-colored heels that cost what it takes to feed a small African child for a Hollywood biopic. I can handle the hallucinogenic mountain before my still bike, but I can't explain why I would want to be with that *one* nerdy man on television; thinking of a real, true, actual (spouting) penis makes me want to wretch on my running Nikes.

There's mood lighting in the spinning-not-spinning-wheel room and I'm too old to be shoving muscles this way and that. I'm too old for a thirty-year-old boy-toy who used to be a Hilfiger model and is definitively prettier than I am and would be turned off by my unshaven winter legs. I want a bubbly bath, a nap, my much older wife. She knows who I am.

Swaddle me in Ben Gay and call me "Baby!"

Telemachus is My Weather Man

Tonight, a silent cirrus covers my nimbus feet: I am soaked in torrents from a 7-day outlook of no, shouldn't, can't, don't, must must must. I pray. For 40 days. I watch as speckled windows transform tea leaves. Refined Earl Grey tests as well as pencils and paper.

I change the channel—click click click. I badmouth an on-going basketball game that keeps me from desperate, disparate distraction. I resent a lumpy pillow that cradles with caution, and three cats, staring, mocking my human emotions. The weather ticker spouts below: Rain. Hard rain. Lightning.

The slight tug of a brewing storm builds in my middle (it's April). Years of didn't and worlds of "Not really?" accompanied by allegorical laughter and a fog of fake matrimony bang on my sensory-soaked bosom. I am Penelope. I have waited for SO long. When my alarm wakes me tomorrow, I will untangle this shroud. I will put on my slicker. I will love.

In the car I wait for ablation and pray for accretion. I know I am a smaller, paler Al Roker lost in a maze or melted by the sun of inspection. I close my eyes at the red light and imagine. I AM. This is real. This has felled my drought. The man behind me, not Odysseus, not the Proci, hammers his horn.

Tiresias: I didn't mean to! I didn't know that I could, or dream that other people did; I held my hands in my lap as tightly as I held my knees together, my heart glued to my sleeve, crazy; I would not understand my own dew point. I was not Fair.

This is my EYE. Tonight, I can see. The past is my Eye Wall.

Rationale

She says, "I can't read this book," and I try not to group her with the other lazy students on campus: the plagiarizers and deadline-skippers, pot heads and procrastinators. She stutters, "I'm a m-m-mother." There is nothing about her body language that signals she is dodging work, or lying, or lost. She has simply found that dark chink in our American armor.

Yes. This book is not for the faint of heart, or those who heart the weak. This book is not to be read aloud, in mixed company, between races or by children. This book was written, I'm sure, because the author had no other choice but to disinfect her memory of the mean MidWest, circa 1930's, its racism and child abuse. It was safe, on paper, but still black and white.

I say, "I see." Because I do. Every*day* I see the pages of that book reenacted. One student, a black woman with gorgeous natural hair, comes to class, her locks suddenly locked straight with heat and carcinogenic formaldehyde, glass-smooth, her contacts blue. She swings her hips and flips that faux Caucasion hair as if she is Aphrodite, not Pecola, and one of us, if we ignore her South African cadence. Men, of course, follow. Another student, known in her country as Da Eun, asks to be called 'Dana.' She tells me this will help her get a job at the local fast food restaurant—now if she could only get rid of her accent. Tammika names her baby "ReJuan," as in "Juan again," because she's 17 and wants her ex-boyfriend who's already moved on to the next naive girl in the next ESL class to see: She's faithful. She's his.

Sara raises her voice from her consistent, South American 2 of 10 to a 6, at least. "Professor, she got raped!" She says this as if this doesn't happen in her country. As if this doesn't happen anywhere on dates, during crimes, within marriages in Lima, only in Lorain, Ohio. She says this as if her country's Catholicism has protected her, with prayers and Pachamama from such, as if the statues in Cuzco have done their jobs and we, Americans, are simply ignorant, faithless.

I know: It won a Nobel prize. It won a Pulitzer.

Her voice drops to a hard-to-hear .5: "But raped. By her father... "

"Yes." *Ari.*

I know—this is not an argument over words; this is not the "Howl" argument I've had a million times over sexuality or vulgarity or someone's misunderstanding of gay male prostitutes in San Francisco. This is disbelief, dire doubt in humanity. I don't know how to tell her, this educated Peruvian woman who holds a Master's in her country and works for minimum wage at Chuck E. Cheese, here: This happened.

This happened in our country, and it happened in our families, and there are children out there who are the product of incest, and there are children in here who think they are worth less than cattle because they don't look like their friends. There are Cholly men, and there are Claudias, too.

All I can do is embrace this woman, and pat away her long-held adoration of us—U.S. She lets me because she is from someplace else.

Booksmarts are Still Silt at the Redneck Riviera

The errant shells from ego breaks are tempest tossed and jagged and cutting; I bleed pain for sharks to heal on this "vacation" with children clamped to my unseasoned (or unseasonable) hips. Glass slipper grains, ground to the size of flossed bikini tops on heavy step-sisters, cover decades of: tanning lotion, sunrise sex, bonfire ash and seaweed. I pry those hardened pricks from my alabaster skin, expose grown-up (read: jiggly) thighs, peel this ass to garish pink beneath a mommy's muumuu, resentful. Diet soda in hand, extra saccharine for sentiment, I swipe some sweat, grit sand in teeth, wonder when he'll tire. I am no sand architect.

While weighty waves threaten XXX-foliation, and the sea washes the shore slate clean, it cannot curb my tongue. I swear with one syllable words (almost inaudible) as the tide rolls over my crab citadel: twelve, now thirteen, now twenty times as my son counts, childishly chronological. My smart son shovels over water foreclosure, hums like a lark with flooding insurance. I've forgotten to apply sunscreen (and patience and fun) and childhood memories, so scale, instead. I am red with emotion, Scarlet (O'Hara).

I shadow smiles, though, of shallow joy, adjacent to perfect spindly legs that will never need Pilates. I dig dig dig with him: heartache, headaches, regrets and regression. I sift wet from dry to castle this fate, as asked. Each time, we are pooled. I am: mother, teacher, wife and sinner. I am missing every other title staring at the pierced navels walking by on trim tummies, watching balding tattoos move on tailored backs. I sow a moat and say I'm sorry.

Like lessons lost in youth, or diluted, dishonest sweat, heat entombs us. The sun falls and falls and hits (beneath this belt, nude). I wait for the temperance of tide and rebirth, my regeneration, or a starfish, four-footed and needing, like me. I count the seconds to "saved" status, wonder if beer works wonders, as I have wandered for more than forty days in a place where I've drowned in clichés: It's hotter than Hades. I do not own a beer can cozy, and there is no lifeguard present. I've misplaced any attention I might have brought home from the hospital with my breast pump.

My child chides only with sanded calves, but my fingernails bleed in borrowed fullness. Below this Cinderella surface are years of draping storms that started with an overbearing mother or a belittling world, hiding all that he wants on six legs. Heaven worms in what waits beyond “me” in echoes of creation crashing. I see; a jellyfish stings my foot, not his. So I call to the less evolved, again. I play my role. Finally, I fish for that one that will feed us all, or the words to hail a fairy godmother.

SECTION THREE: LOVINGKINDNESS

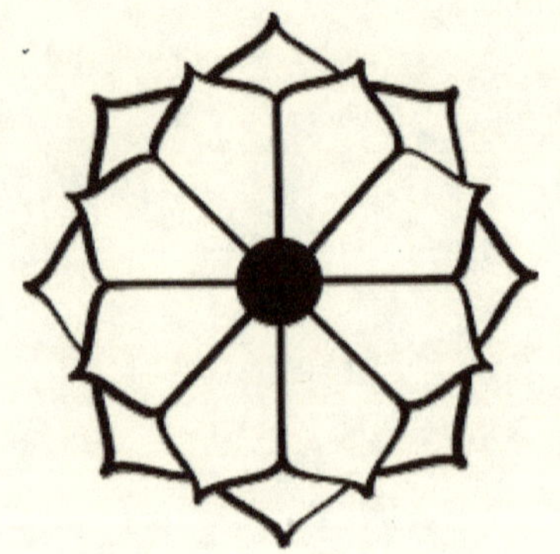

Mommy Diet

For Kelly

Surely peanut butter M&Ms count as protein in a diet where one is trying to shrink a marsupial pocket of two C-section babies without putting plastic surgery on a maxed out credit card. Candy can help lift a tired rear off the puppy-pee stained carpet, at least enough to walk to the PTA meeting three blocks away. I admit, we eat them because we want to look better than the other mothers whose running schedules are never impacted by their children, and we are more emotional than logical when the scale hits 130. They're rich and beautiful and selfish, those other moms, and they have nannies and home managers and summer places in countries below the equator. These are women who enjoy Brazilian waxes and caviar and the tug of a new facelift against the foreskin of a just-legal lawn care professional.

Surely the sugar is fine—it's natural—and I am a natural woman, given that I stay at home, work, work online at home, nap in the soccer field parking lot, text too much and write my every move up on Facebook for a virtual room of possible past friends or possibly lying admirers to follow like a trail of trash guts from my spotless kitchen to the begrunged outdoor can—with a child on my widening hip. I'm natural like the sex I rarely have because my two possum pups need more at night, clawing at my back and that monkey, than during the daylight hours at school where I pay logic-teetering tuition for a stand-in mommy to teach A, B, C's and geometry, Greek myths, situational ethics and playground insider trading.

The candy coating must be protection from germs: cold, flu, Rota, vomit-in-a-straight-stream-across-the-room (unless you are in mommy's bed, then on her pillow, square). The color is for the seasonally disturbed, too, combating gray depression in dye made to whittle frown lines, though not as well as Restalyne or that new reality show where everyone is fatter than you.

The "M"s stand for "mighty": This is the way you might feel when you make it through a home aerobic workout dvd without a child crying, falling, pooping, or the phone ringing, a fireman asking for money you don't have for a volunteer hero you'll probably never see. You can buy jelly, too, he says; but they don't have sugar-free. If you're not mighty, you're morbidly obese and just hurt from side lunges.

Maybe "M" is for "me time," where you have dinner with friends in restaurants with foreign names and drinks with salted rims and adult conversation about politics, literature, the news that is not the letter of the day on "Sesame Street" or an upcoming super hero series or an episode of that four-year-old Canadian whose mother never raises her voice and whose sister never places chewed gum in her squeaky clean baby duck hair. This is a dinner that is often cut short because the baby has an ear infection, the-sister-in-law can't stay past eleven, the spouse is yawning with half a beer stoking REM cycles and curtailing libido.

The other "M"? Marriage. There is a reason you chose all of this, and it isn't because stretch marks are "in," or flab is the new black, or children, when washed and brushed and dressed in designer clothes that can only be bought online from a Parisian boutique, are the new Kate Spade bags. You got married because you had that ideal image of someone who would love you, for better or worse. You never imagined the worse, or the way a hot 30-something might look in nine years without a gym membership, but it ebbs and flows with the elementary school calendar and the head lice epidemics, and she loves you anyway. She would kiss that off-center abdominal scar—if there was time—and certainly will when the children go off to college or you forget her name in the throes of genetic disorders.

Forget You... and Forget Me, too, Cee Lo

At first, it's almost amusing to take him out; watching a grown man dry-hump a five-foot tall feline releases the giggles in even the most integrity-stricken and empathic: Congress. Sure, people stare, but these are people you'll never see outside of that Pet Smart, that Saturday morning; these are people who've just adopted their seventh dog or a sickly, $500 saltwater fish, and you feel above them, somehow, as you once did the role-playing marching band members in high school. You do not explain the burgeoning neurological symptoms to the sixteen year old Mormon cashier who fingers her cross at his kitty climax; you would not take that kind of time (or pleasure) away from him in this state, or your weekend errand schedule with said father. Besides, he'll leave a large donation in the plastic cat's head (via social security), as well as his crumpled up phone number—from 1978. The next time you take him pet food shopping, the next time you're in town, you'll simply hold his hand or belt loop, as a leash is cruel and unusual and those safety backpacks with handles they make for kids in pedophile-filled malls just don't come in his size, even online.

After a few maternally mauling weekends of pet food shopping, and several ripped belt loops, you'll realize your life will never be the same, as you, having abstained from procreation and faithfully taken Depo Provera for decades to keep the world from sinful overpopulation, will still have a sixty-something year old child to keep—with your sister. You'll bathe him and dress him and feed him and scrub his sheets clean when his mental clarity is lacking, every other weekend. You'll see it's ironic, this parenting shift, in the way the word "driveway" is ironic to linguists, or the way overweight women order a Diet Coke with their Big Mac and fries: ridiculous and sad, something akin to drowning in a sink. Standing. This man, once a charming womanizer you wouldn't talk to for his raised eyebrows and lolling tongue behind your mother's back, is now a stone of a sexual being—simply dead weight—and cannot remember your mother's front with help or a name tag. You'll stop taking him to Pet Smart at all on your weekends, not because people stare at his antics, but because you cannot look at his face wondering if it is your future.

The Runaway

Your mother: "You cannot tunnel to China without looking back!" No ma'm, not without a black passport, and not if you've chosen to better your breaks in this animal's life. You need: silver-plated spoons, salted caramels, a second pair of underwear. You need clear directions.

Somehow, yard-by-yard, mineral wisdom seeps in through reaching, raking fingertips, through root vegetables and retaining walls; there is no room for monkey-back rides in barefoot and burdened Buddhist (?) Beijing. You must unload your grief before....

Halfway to the core, you curse the crust, the fuss of emotions. You look for your center, a snake. You see: He was a myth to the masses, most under twelve; now he is ten years gone, yet gilded. Your mother still celebrates his birthday; you still cry to "Danny Boy." The Dharma doesn't offer drugs or doctors of psychology.

You think of terra cotta warriors who surely ward off wakes. But he was that pancake batter maker, Bisquick creator, and, if that 'if' equals 'then,' he also turned into the Aztec sun god at daybreak, danced

Irish jigs on table tops, broke his own bitty finger to hold a golf club best; this is middle school math, and karma.

On our mantle—in it, too—there is a picture: He often shadowboxed when the heavy weight of the world would heave-ho, not let go, Bartleby itself on his two shoulders, one angel, one angle. He studied the sport at night, by radio, driving a Pepsi truck away from his peppered past. Prescriptions don't pause.

Tenzin knows he pencil-pushed his way through *Times* crossword puzzles; you scrape the outer core for access, also hampered by a sixth grade education. He perfected pizza crusts, sullied by greedy partners and a state seeped in lefse and lutefisk, littered in shotgun shells and deer carcasses. Your inner core aches, agnostic.

This heat cannot be helped, or measured. He took me golfing three months before he died, no handicap but carving cancer. This man glimmers brighter than Chinese New Year, offers satori; my childhood tunnel collapses. I call for calm, my mudra, in "Mom!"

Keaton

I loved you for ten days before I knew of you, or the way your hormones would interact with mine, worry me, excite me, cause me to vomit in gross amounts.

I loved you a whole 70 days before I bled, bled buckets in bed, in the middle of the night, my partner states away and rushing to make a red-eye home.

I loved you for 98 days before I recognized those turning feelings to be contractions, before the doctors ordered me to stay in bed, and friends urged me to stand on my head, so precious you were to all of us....

I loved you for 140 days before we knew you were a girl, before we knew our spiritual emails and texts and tweets had been answered.The universal Facebook status read: "Female Blessing." God and Buddha had worked together to give us one yin, one yang.

I loved you for 266 days before I ever knew you.

(She loved you for 266 days, too.)

The Cosbys We are Not

There is no "fun" in "dysfunction" when blood bickers at 1200 miles—ten cents a minute—and holiday gatherings mean verifying that, via nose shape and medically-approved DNA stripe, you are who your mother always said you were, and your father cannot deny it any longer. Your unruly hair could stand-in for your late grandmother's bush, and your brother's eyebrows are unmistakable Brown family bristle. You pop a Prozac.

And you do what you have to do, what is expected from you as the One Who Fits Least. You break out the *Cooking Light* and brazenly brave the world of vegetarian fare for a meat-lover's fete. You know your brother will ignore your culinary muse; he will bring burgers from some drive-thru manned by Mexicans used to missing Catholic holy days, used to being maligned and mocked for mediocre English. He will bring liquor, too, from the always-lit Jews' store on the corner; they will heckle and whisper, "Mr. Jesus," as he waits for that brown paper bag, not knowing your brother subscribes to Mr. Buddha and Jose Cuervo, alone, despite his WASP waltzing.

You'll call a dozen other Browns, holding both your tongue and ethical breath, and offer free sustenance for once-a-year civility. Some will be thrilled to be invited at all, because the last time they drove the three hours to your home they drank too much, mooned the room, outed an aunt and nicknamed the newest addition "Troll Baby." Some will screen their calls, first, as seeing their own last name on the caller I.D. means a future funeral, an expected engagement gift, a loan collection or divorce pity party. But eventually they will pick up; family guilt runs thick when newly-born or newly-risen Christian myths loom.

You will be patient as you cross off names; "How many are coming?" really means, "Are you and your on again-off again, squirrel-killing fiancé joining us? Or is it just you and the unruly, out-of-wedlock kids?" Your sister-in-law isn't stupid—her IQ is at least 70 and she knows enough to have a pregnant friend pee on the pregnancy test she threatens her fickle man with—she just prefers to keep the family in suspense about her nocturnal emission adventures, as well as who she might be dating behind the baby daddy's back. She, also, prefers you don't mention her tremendous weight gain or weighty new tits. She says "Four," but leaves out names.

You will tell everyone, "2 o'clock," and know that, playing telephone against the tick tock of Brown time, this request will be muted or misinterpreted or simply ignored. The many genetically-linked pairs of retrieving ears belong to strange and once-estranged individuals who don't care when you'll be dressed, showered, or the tofu ham and turkey finished. They only hear the answer to, "Will there be beer?" They only care if cards with money will be exchanged.

At 11:52, that day, your mother-in-law will *tsssk* the sad turn of titillating events before they even begin. She will say to one daughter, "In my day, mothers did not wear thongs." Pause. Smoke an unfiltered cigarette despite her oxygen tank. "They didn't give blow jobs in public, either." To which the other sister, the one who's been married four times and has never had to change her last name (one brother, a cousin, and two uncles later, she uses the same monogrammed fingertip towels from her first marriage) will explain, "Dark alleys aren't 'public,' mother." You will turn your back to hide your laugh and seal the tailored veggie gel with rum glaze.

The phone will ring (1:45); the youngest brother-by-marriage will be late. He is busy snorting coke or spanking a prostitute he met in Canada when the ice fishing holes were too cold for skinny-dipping. He will call from his cell, drunk: "I'll be there at three, I swear. I'll bring the fuckin' dip, okay?" He, of course, will mean tobacco. Your father-in-law will take his fake teeth out in wild anticipation, seemingly unaware of the calendar date: Easter. He will gleefully gum a Pillsbury roll; his wife will roll her eyes.

At two o'clock the table will be set with crystal rabbits, Faberge eggs, and other appropriate statuettes of springtime animals NOT mating or wounded by a four-year-old toting a hunting rifle or molested by the very distant delegates from West Virginia. You will say hello to all versions of sinners and saints over contemporary images of one iconic lamb: (cheap) hookers, drug-addled cousins, the brother who drinks too much, the mother who knows it and ignores it, the great-grandmother who grew up in a Catholic orphanage, and you—the lone lesbian who does not believe that African Americans are "colored foreigners" or that Muslims should be banned from public office. You are the one who created THIS meal, and you are yet ostracized.

So you will pour wine seconds before your sister-in-law (who WILL bring her Hell's Angel fiancé, but will not wear her engagement or Nuva rings) can kiss your cheek or pass out her best friend's sonogram picture and list last year's best baby names. There will be a moment—less than a minute—of grace:

Holding hands around a food-filled table signals the start of the feeding frenzy.

Before hands are dropped, or elderly pants, it will begin to rain outside, syncing nature with your slowly sinking sanity. This will be a fine finish to that day. You know: Rain (RAIN) can wash away watercolors on hidden eggs, muddy footprints on the porch, soft feces from visiting animals with bellies full of fatty gravy, and Martha Stewart visions of meringue peaks. But as a premonition of your brother breaking out the mandatory Milwaukee's Best surfaces, you will think: Sometimes family ties are meant for hanging.

Same Sutures

For Elizabeth Huff

Wounds:

1) From the street, the house is sigh-brown, its shutters limp and light from rain, and ruddy. Ruined. It's been three years since she's known this house she kept for fifty. (One demand: "What is today's date? Our location?" Silence.)

2) From the sidewalk, she's more than brusque and blonde, more than business: Hospital heels click, chiming seconds to China doll children in hair bows and bow-tied tennis shoes. Theirs are scents of lavender and baby lotion.

To Prevent Infection:

1) At the front door, beyond the gauzy window veils, she mind maps in her worn, velveteen chair: scribbles half-names of mother, father, siblings, children. The chair is all that's left of him; the map is all that's left. Even a rabbit knows: Lying to one's self is still lying.

2) In the living room, she kicks off her professional façade, peels off stockings of Other People's Needs,

and germs you cannot fight alone. She's "Mom," now; she's "Wife," stripped to common nouns and casual clothes. Soon, she'll scrub her face to plain, pale, spent.

Hemostasis:

1) The kitchen's fogged in family time. The table is set in "Beaver" fashion; she can recall 1957. Her daughter means well, Teresa-reminds her: Yes, you like beef. You like green beans. Eyedropper in elderly eye corners: He's just coming home from work, now.

2) She holds a mustard jar ajar. Drops it on a slate floor. In cleaning up, she slits her pointer finger open, like an important piece of mail, a summons with directions. Her son cries, cringes at the smatter on the Samsung fridge. Stainless steel is stained in red.

Epidermis:

1) She moves to sleep—she sleeps so much these days. But all she can do is stare. The photographs on the wall are nothings, abstracts. Her memories are mute, and the (even knowledgeable) doctor cannot mega-phone them. She curls up around: soft, square, smell, *this*.

2) Eleven stitches = one and one. Together. Fixed. So many years pares the bed to a quarter. She throws one leg atop a leg not hers. She is a lowercase "H"; her wife sits on a thigh, sated, breathing (synchronized) as they could never do in daylight.

Bandages:

1) Aricept, nurse, prayer.

2) Layers of blankets. Love.

A Pattern Unworthy of Westminster Cathedral

Above an old fireplace littered with cold ash, and near a pane where time's lost in still pictures, there are: past loves and fickle failures and virtual safety and piece-s. There are years-old candies and fingered demands on dusty shelves. There is one, crumbling mosaic. I know antiquity at thirty-four, or at least my ovaries do; I've lived before. Now I rest, flashing hot, on a single nail of pause. I wait for breath.

My green, tricked in tarnished brass, stirs eco-friendly rules. My son has learned what I've wanted: recycling and composting, compassion and Buddha. Now, he believes I throw too many things away, should save my crusts for starving children, need to treasure the shards of grass-colored glass from the goblet I hurled against the wall in a fit of passion; there was no passion that night, the night before, the month before that. Earthly Zoloft tempers those highs. I clean scattered obscenity; "Mommy, we can make a picture frame." Yes. We can historicize that holiday where my hair was frizzy and my thighs were flouncy and my sister-in-law asked if I had any pants (too small for me) that she could borrow to wear with her Santa sweater?

This blue is tired and a tad too 18th century Danish for the mood that I'm in when the DVR misses my show about other housewives who are more fucked up, clinically, than the ones I know, but also have the money for a regular babysitter and personal chefs and direly needed therapists—sex or not. It's muted, like when the television decides it must save energy, too, or the dishwasher ends its day without a final rinse stage (ornery from being so taken advantage of) or the cat has thrown up on the wood floor again, stealth. This blue is the color of my eyes when I can't find the Visine and the baby's top teeth have decided to break in—bold—and I am alone in my king-sized bed. This color was once my Something Borrowed, now something torn. This blue is "Dream House Shutter" blue, Behr, too.

Red bleeds through like strawberry stains on white t-shirts, or other natural seeds on cotton sheets on Sunday mornings, pre-kids; it purses like missed lips around the edges of: pushing past that four mile marker, panting for that baby, breaking promises, lacking so much. The crimson tickles tainted memories of when I loved and ignored, or loved but refused, claimed I couldn't, or lusted and did all three. It's fist-sized and ticks, keeps tethered time, skips, however non-chronological. It paints why and how I am here, belittles standing still, kisses me with ruby slipper truth, and accepts me with garish faults. Spells: VULVA, and LOVE, and shadowboxes SIN. Outlines what I do not want to express, and what seeps out, regardless.

I am all of these broken tiles, precariously balanced a-bove a yellowing (faux) sheepskin rug. But, together with you, I am whole.

A Businesswoman, a Poet, and a Bottle Attachment

"Three in a boat!" she shouts, waving wedding rings in side-straddled eights. This boat is tempest-tossed and touched with moss, leaks. Charon rows with sub-par sticks. Yet this is fate. This is the world's most unfair question.

You married your spouse to seal spouts together; you courted. Then came baby, not quite bouncing, not quite quiet. The new triad tricks what seemed a perfect pair, what seemed unsinkable, and salt water sanitizes once-messy passion with one sea contraction.

Even soaked, spouse equals strong, stronger than you, a chance at survival—for two. But throwing an equal overboard, besides being physically tough, means tagging the tangible evidence of your love "recyclable." Not doing so means watching a war wash across mother's face: slap, sting, sulfur rising from the Dead.

A child is weak, and wan, and meek. One and one, grown, weighted with splattered "rights," (and wrongs), restless nights, equals this mean in a marriage with dependents too dependent to swim, too precious to sink, forgotten. This is trust; this is Tabula Rasa. Erasing such means erasing all, a soothsayer says.

The answer is? There is no bathwater, here, in the home of the halves.

Gidget's Unrest

Having woken up at 3 am for a girl's date avec (non-alcoholic) bottle with my infant daughter, I was solidly asleep when something real and warm (tangible) patted my newly pedi'd peds at seven that morning. I shut my eyes, not caring if the cat had wandered in with a well-loved (or humped or stuffing-less) stuffed animal, or if the elderly dog had passed out on my ankles in a narcoleptic/dementia-induced/possible puppy Prozac fit. Not caring if I was a Scrooge for ignoring pertinent pet needs. I pulled the blankets over my head, pressed my eyelids together against the blossoming, allergenic world, and gave in to the wormy feeling of lack of blood to my toes.

Unfortunately, a heavy throat clearing accompanied the patting, and the smell of Earl Grey tea primed my senses for waking against my best motherly interests. I tentatively opened one eye—a slit—and slyly scanned the bed for animals with vegetables or minerals or libidos abound. What I saw was not an animal, per se.

I'd wondered what God would look like, of course. I'd sat in church while holding tightly to sacraments of sangha and wondered if God was, in fact, a bald and toweled monk in orange, a peaceful flame of non-fiction for the troubled: Tenzin Gyatso. And here she was. Too much like Sally Field to shake the maternal feel, too Gidget-cute to want to kiss; she was too sweet to ignore, even as I was addict-tired. I wondered if there were Academy Awards in Heaven and, if so, what those statues looked like, what happened to those who forgot to mention their spouses in their thank you's, if there were any losers in the "Supporting Actress" category.

"Drink," she said, stripped to verbs, like a Hemingway character with some ugly secret hidden in elephant-hunting metaphors. I closed my one, pirated eye. Another hand tickled the baby gray hairs sprouting zig-zag on the crown of my non-regal head.

The other, hair-tending voice said, "Namaste."

Now. I am not the kind of woman who would allow hallucinations to guide her everyday life. I am not the kind of person who believes that God—in Sally Field's metaphysical bodysuit—and Buddha would bother to visit my home, some favored woman in a sea of saints. I decided I'd finally crossed over into the world of clinical lack of sleep. I'd finally gone insane, or died in my hour of rest, or been drugged by the neighbor who scowls when my normally indoor cat jumps the backyard fence and sprays his begonia bush with arrogance. I began to pray.

I prayed that my often situational ethics would hold holy water, at least for Peter's consultation, and that my good will over the course of my willed life would stand at least as good a chance in Heaven (or my new body) as my last will and testament would in court, being my wife was never my legal wife and my country is eons behind my morals. I prayed in a way that seemed logical, because I didn't know the tried and true Catholic version of asking God, someone, anyone, for help:

"Sally Field, who is on the edge of my bed—dressed—hallowed be thy media'd past. Thy teenaged-body fallen, thy movies Blockbuster'd, in Hollywood as in my town-by-the-water.

God and Buddha give me, this forsaken morning, the ability to stand. And forgive me for the times I have: pretended to be asleep so my spouse would tend to the baby, wished for bigger boobs, wished for smaller—though much higher—breasts, had too much wine in inappropriate company, loved the wrong person, loved the right person the wrong way, built a dream on a raincloud, hoped for it to rain on someone else's parade, hoped to be trampled by the parade, hoped to have a parade in my honor, lacked confidence and stolen another's, forgotten balance and trust and my blessings, and Siddhartha. Forgive me for wanting more than the kings of third world countries have at any given moment and giving nothing in return; forgive me for holding out, and putting out, and allowing my emotions to run out into the highway of society. I am not perfect."

Sally Field said, I have given my youth for you.

Buddha reminded: Progress, not perfection.

My daughter stirs the radio waves from her room to my monitor. "I cannot die," I admit. "I have too much to lose."

A Radical Proposal

They—a pious and political plural—say we (just two) cannot be married. Some say it is because our bodies don't fit together, in the way tab A fits into slot C (with salve), but they have never seen you comfort me. They have never seen you curl your strength around my core, offer courage via osmosis and hope through transdermal application. They have been blind to everything but our sex lives, and we are not nearly so buck wild.

Some say this—you and I—are unnatural. It's true; there are days when I wear make-up, straighten my hair, wear man-made material, even pick up dinner at the inorganic drive-thru. I always wear glasses. So I offer these natural men and women, these biblical rule-followers: Splenda for their coffee, their tea, and jiggers of vodka. I offer them birth control and DVRs. I offer them gastric bypasses, plastic surgery, chemotherapy and Viagra.

They say that legal church bonding has always been between X and Y (for that ten minute in-and-out) and this is history, and history is sacred. I ask them, then, and beg them not on blow-jobbing knees, but my bottoming back, to consider marriage between races, and an individual's ability to divorce without being hanged. I ask them to rethink owning people, and to tell men that their wives are not cattle, cannot be beaten, cannot be made to "obey" with a hot poker or a poking appendage.

They whisper that God doesn't recognize us, or our love, but surely HE is not so far-sighted. I wonder if Yahweh, if Allah, if Vishnu, if Bahgwaan or Krishna can see this: the weighty political wars. And if they cannot, does it mean we don't exist?

Shadow People Still

Once, when the world was flat, and women couldn't vote, I knew you: dark, quiet, a bottom with few words but "Yes," and "Sure," the vernacular of the bartering broken and furrowing few under a black sky whispering soul songs.

You wouldn't raise your eyes to mine, then, and you couldn't leave my land, tethered as you were by the cadence of culture. This was when it was legal to beat your wife on six continents, force her to have sex with you, then divorce her because she didn't conceive that coveted child, but gaggles of girls. This: greasy fingerprints on canonized crystal.

Once, Galileo was kept, and we all agreed; we killed the Jews because they, too, were dark and not our kind. (They grew no wheat…) We stoned a woman to death because she dared fall in love, and we carved our daughters with scythes so they wouldn't feel love at all when they married. You (YOU) slept on bales of hay unbefitting a baby Jesus and your wrists stung with the seal of someone else's name.

This was when genocide was comfortable: Aboriginals, Cherokees, Dzungars, Assyrians, Tibetans. This was when we learned that AIDS was real; we learned death could follow us in a needle or needed bottle, a fuzzy drive, a telephone pole plastered with "Missing" fliers of missed and ministered youth. You worked as hard as me, made pennies, paid into a system that practiced, but not what it should have preached.

Now, you are still. You are still dark, quiet, seen but not heard; your voice is tagged as misogynistic, your women easy, your men jailbirds. You are chained, choked by images: fried chicken, collard greens, watermelon. All this, and the world is round.

Roger Ebert: Two Thumbs Down

If I had a million dollars, bundled up in sateen sheets, cuddled with righteous rubber bands that never once held Ziplocs over worried mouths or pricks, or held crack, tight, like a wanted child in the arms of an "infertile" woman, if I had those bills cleaned of bodily fluids and made from Godly goods, I would not give them, exchange them, beguile other humans with them for a place on a list of 200,000 Chosen Ones. Wile E. Coyote may trick a roadrunner, but not this desert wanderer.

If I had 80,659,970 yen, packed in pickle jars and Styrofoam peanuts beneath pine planks in a dilapidated shed, I would not build a bomb shelter, or hoard bottled spring water, store canned goods in a below-ground room with room for four—and the family pets. I cannot swallow a story of salvation through a church savings account any more than I will the salt from a part in the Red Sea on my virgin margarita at a hole-y all-night diner; I cannot Camp.

683,000 Euros would be much better spent training volunteers to teach the open and mindful illiterate, to bring water to those without cups, to make meals for the immovable, mentally fragile, jobless and Job-like. It would spay an ark of animals, treat a tribe of lepers to Mother Teresa salve, and bring Bibles, Korans, and Bhagavad-Gitas to faith-full-y desperate girls in boys' worlds, girls who may never feel love the way they should—whole, as created, crowned with natural nerves by a universal hand that carved equality into an apple tree long before Family Radio Talk wrote salvation rules.

I could use 836,200 Swiss francs to save myself... or not.

For the Masses Who Choose Spiked Kool-Aid

"Eat your waffle, baby," spooling like lamb's wool from the front seat of a mommy-van hoping for some sanity after the private school drop-off. "But I'm not hungry," and mewling, from an under-forty-pound booster smack dab in the rearview mirror, on repeat. Some political pouting crashes a normal pop station of two-minute teeny bopper songs where "fuck," as a verb, is bleeped for baby ears that, somehow, are obliged to hear casualty numbers from the not-too-far East (that are fucking depressing) and the anonymity-challenged insist, confess conjugal time in 9-5 prisons where "open-doored" means more than obvious complaining about female management. DJs sympathize. Everything, here, equals a domestic morning, the rest of the world at a levied, and government-supported, bay.

A red light rakes 100,000 miles of road-tested resistance: lift the right foot, glide, slow. Stomp! Stop. Near-vacant vehicles nudge the yellow lines like DUI numbers, sift through traffic as sand in a wet sieve. Sitcom images from some solitary Saturday night replay, reckless, with lack of focused (or moving) meditation on a dead dashboard. A phone rings with rhetoric: "No, sure, that's fine," when it isn't, or shouldn't be—can't be today, of all days. This phrase cradles confidence like a bird's nest swinging, dipping into rocking breezes only breaths away from a black snake whose babies, also, need to eat.

She nods, she taps fingertips on a gearshift. Once, we were high schoolers; now, we, like snakes, are expected to shed—other people, inconsiderates, the young at mouth. We are directed to molt, quietly. "I mean it!" heckles and hassles, and honesty faints. Cell phone off speaker: Cells fall soft. Punctuation bleeds through. There are pieces of torn cinnamon Eggos splattered like semen throughout the back-seat, but no condoms, no passion.

Ten minutes from cycling dishes and diaper changing, laughing in an absolute lack of leftover estrogen or viable eggs, advertising angels steer this sweaty, sleepy woman to a startling line for expensive beans, steeped (and not even in Stoli). She is under par in scandal; she's swathed in yoga pants and a vacation tee from someone else's vacation: period panties, sports bra, not showered, not make-upped. And still, she wants... She wants. Waiting, waiting, waiting out her wanting, she thinks: Today is the first day of...

Brittany K. Fonte

There is no end; there is no echo. From child-pasted sidewalks, scenes like a mosaic glued without Ativan: "But only if you can," means "I'll ask again if you do this time," and, "Hello," translates to: "Hello," but also, "Gained some weight?" "My child's smarter than yours," even, "Check out Ritalin, girl. He needs it." Sure, soul sister. Finally, coffee. Namaste.

Time and Tide

Love hangs somewhere between They'll Never Find Out and It'll Break Me. It's slip-knotted, slack between a leaning apple tree and a rusted flagpole, twisting, turning blue, toes just inches off the ground. It's desperate. This space is Mississippi, or the defendant's desk at the Nuremberg Trials: wanting.

Secrets are holes in otherwise moth-eaten garments, decades old, unfashionable now as they were when worn. They are limp, holding onto sanity with old-fashioned clothespins, giving in to gravity, gravity. Once spoken, once agreed to, secrets drip onto just-turned soil. They stain like garden gloves grieving the coming winter, warming rare bulbs.

Old women scrub their souls on washboards, beat their regrets on ragged rocks until they fade. When this doesn't work, they give in to love, to dirt.

Why Prose Poetry?

When people ask, more thoughtless than not, Why prose poetry? I tell them, Just like basic Algebra, or at least addition and subtraction (and maybe multiplication—which is why we have Sex Ed) there are several solid "real world" applications for such. They balk, of course, and ask how I live off of lines that don't even rhyme in a time of Dr. Seuss nostalgia and online sales of Beatles' paraphernalia. Then, because I cannot prove to people who've never been moved by a d.a. levy musing, or been made love to by a seriously hung sonnet, or cried to the truth of Sapphire in a barred window pane, that education for the sake of education is what separates the scholars from the downtown ballers-for-booze, I am bold as "Bump its" on *'Shore* Snookie. I offer:

Ransom Notes. Surely your average filthy rich parent has an appreciation and often pot-induced remembrance of "Howl" in a hard-hitting Contemporary Lit class—the one with the hot professor who never wore panties and always sat on the desk in front of the class, legs crossed like Sharon Stone when she wasn't famous enough to wear lingerie in films. The spoken word feel of an appeal for a bank account's bills must seem more real than the magazine cut-outs from the movies you see on Pay-Per-View (when you'd rather be watching porn.)

Baby Announcements. When you want to detract from the new arrival via your teenaged daughter and some oily guy she met while on vacation in Ocean City, or your "darling" tramp and your (criminal) ex-boyfriend who, unfortunately, had a thing for younger girls and not just older ones acting a character in a Disney television show in their daughter's mini skirts, prose poetry is the way to go. Imagine the lyrics to a sexually-charged, yet redundant, pop-song atop an electric blue (that won't wash the baby out in the pastel wrap against the cheetah-print bra) background. You can even give the baby a symbol—like Prince—and then, if the baby turns out illiterate like its mysterious father (or *Maury* set of fathers), he or she will still be able to sign into rehab, alone.

Dear John letters. Think distraction, here. You don't want to come off as the flaming bitch in your 100-word sign-off to your one time bed buddy via tweet or status update or emoticon-filled text; he or she might have attractive friends. With jobs. And after all, they were hot enough to make out with in the line at Starbucks (for the heterosexuals), or the check out at Pet Smart (for our lesbian friends), or at the meth party-come-"gym" (for our pretty boys). This temporary temperature raising (even weeks ago) means you owe it to them to at least craft a lyrical let go. Besides, these losers will love a "goodbye" akin to a Stevie Nicks' song on change and moving on (add image of falling rocks, here).

Notes to your children's teachers (when they've been suspended for cherry bombs in the public toilets, or sending naked pictures of themselves to the new music teacher, or hacking into the computer system to fail all the jocks for the weekly wedgies) can benefit from some poetic license, too. What teacher doesn't appreciate a well-written note that uses punctuation correctly, then applauds his or her work with creative similes and metaphysical compliments? If the teacher happens to be an English teacher, this apology for your child's lethargy or antipathy can, also, double as an extra credit assignment on the intricacies of rhythm and internal rhyme in contemporary American literature.

Finally, and obviously, if you are less attractive than the average A-lister, and you can no longer stand dating the chromosomally abnormal (or accident prone) Subway sandwich maker, prose poems are excellent additives for your 900 number calls. Somehow, the women who answer the phones find comfort in the fact that men (and women) can still string together a line of iambic pentameter in the times of "No Child Left Behind," and rocketing tuition costs, and parental job loss. It isn't easy navigating a higher education system in the midst of economic heresy, but one-time hookers whose breasts have fallen to hip level and whose all-nighter tips have been lost altogether, certainly salivate over such work, and may give you their home addresses for some mighty meter. They know.

Acknowledgments

My most humble gratitude belongs to my better half, who put me through graduate school and believed in my work when I couldn't believe in myself, who loved me through my lows and brought me ice cream by the pint to soothe, who has given me hope in its highest form: our children.

I thank Matt Ryan for pushing me to continue writing when my parental duties grew and I felt I had nothing left; you are a dear friend, a fabulous editor, and I love you.

Christopher: You have not only been my editor, but my friend. The belief you show in me is beyond what I could have ever dreamed. You are a kind and beautiful soul. Thank you.

I could not have accomplished this collection without my supportive and thoughtful mentor, K.L. Cook.

Eric, Kathleen, Regie: Your sweet words bring tears to my eyes.

Kelly, you are such an amazing friend. Thank you for being my shoulder to cry on and my partner in crime.

I thank my parents and my brother, too, for helping me to see anything is possible.

And to all of you whom I haven't mentioned by name, who have read drafts and given feedback and trolled websites for my name, you are in my heart.

About the Author

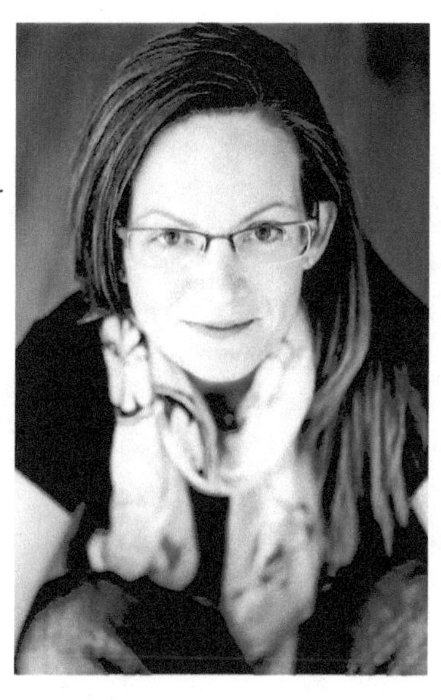

Brittany K. Fonte holds an MFA in Creative Writing, Fiction. Her work, both fiction and poetry, can be found in literary journals like *Breadcrumb Scabs*, *Literary Mama*, *42 Opus*, etc. Currently, Brittany edits fiction for *Best New Writing* and poetry for Low Brow Press. She teaches composition and fiction/nonfiction writing at the university level, as well as dabbles in the D.C. slam poetry scene. Brittany lives with her partner and two children in Annapolis, Maryland, and is working on a prose poetry collection about the 1980s.

www. BrittanyKFonte.com

www.ingramcontent.com/pod-product-compliance
Lightning Source LLC
La Vergne TN
LVHW091004080826
845145LV00003B/1126

* 9 7 8 1 9 3 3 4 3 5 4 2 8 *